"Every pastor, faith formation direct[or]
leads in a parish—should read *Enga[ge* ...]
of experience, and, even more impor[tantly, passion for engaging families in] faith, to this work. Her insights are enhanced by her easily accessible writing, and while she grounds the principles, practices, and ideas she offers in research and the best practices of parish leaders, she invites each reader to draw on his or her own experience and dream of parish life anew." ■ **LEISA ANSLINGER**

"Many parishes struggle to engage families and keep them connected to the life of the Church. In her new book, Denise Utter provides a creative and accessible framework for parish outreach to families in all stages of faith. Replete with practical examples, grounded theologically in Scripture, and anchored by her life experience, this book is a must-read for all those in parish ministry." ■ **JULIANNE STANZ**, *Director of Discipleship and Parish Life, Diocese of Green Bay*

"Denise Utter sees the future of faith formation. In *Engage Every Family*, she digs into the key lessons learned from the disruption of the pandemic and harvests an abundance of hopeful principles and strategies that are creating the next iteration of Catholic faith formation. Read this book, and you will come away with renewed hope for faith formation and a packed toolbox for building the vision." ■ **JIM MERHAUT**, *Founder of Coaching to Connect*

"We don't need the numerous research studies to tell us that this isn't the 1980s or even the 2000s. We're experiencing it—a whole new world. What we did in the past won't work/isn't working today. Real-life stories, practical examples, and multiple resources provide concrete steps of how to start and how to keep building a faith formation process that engages, empowers, and energizes for every family. This is an invaluable and indispensable book for every catechetical leader and catechist—not for their bookshelves, but constantly at their fingertips." ■ **JANET SCHAEFFLER, OP**

"Denise Utter has been an award-winning pioneer and innovator on the forefront of family faith formation. In this book, she offers families and faith leaders sound theory, superb motivation, and innovative, diverse strategies—all grounded in practice and refinement—to help move us all onward to renewal in faith formation. Her commitment to engaging and equipping others in this important task is a great source of hope and vibrancy for our Church." ■ **MIKE PATIN,** *Catholic speaker and author*

"Denise presents a modern approach to Catholic disciple making (faith formation) that is rooted in the radical and real accompaniment ministry style of Jesus. An approach where Catholic doctrine and tradition is celebrated alongside the authentic lived experience of today's Catholic family."
■ **KATIE NEU,** *Program Manager, San Pedro Spiritual Development Center*

"Denise Utter has provided the Church a great gift in this practical, balanced, leading-edge exploration on this vital topic. It offers a vision and pathway for 'internal' evangelization and pastoral renewal. Every parish needs to get a copy of *Engage Every Family* and reimagine faith formation with it as a resource!" ■ **TOM QUINLAN**

"Filled with stories, examples, and practical wisdom, this book guides pastors and faith formation leaders in creating parish communities that can meaningfully engage families and nurture their faith at home. Every parish wants to involve families and help them grow in faith. *Engage Every Family* provides you with ideas and strategies that can actually work in parishes of all sizes and shapes, illustrated by real-world parish examples. Don't just read this book. Use it as your guide to making family faith formation a reality in your parish— starting right now!" ■ **JOHN ROBERTO,** *Lifelong Faith Associates*

"The challenge of engaging families in the faith formation of their children is on the hearts and minds of most every forward-thinking parish. Denise Utter's book *Engaging Every Family: A Parish Guide to Integrated Faith Formation* is a comprehensive, thought-provoking, and rich resource for any parish leader who cares about engaging families. Denise gives the reader background to communicate the need for innovation in faith formation. She offers a variety of examples to consider and implement. The material combines relevant ideas with innovative and current strategies. This book will be a valuable resource for parish leaders. It informs and inspires a hopeful vision for a pressing and important topic vital to the future of the Church." ■ **DR. KATHIE AMIDEI**

Sr. Janet,
Thank you for inspiration, mentorship, accompaniment. So grateful for your encouragement.
Love, Denise

ENGAGE EVERY FAMILY

A Parish Guide to Integrated Faith Formation

DENISE UTTER

TWENTY-THIRD PUBLICATIONS
twentythirdpublications.com

Twenty-Third Publications
One Montauk Avenue, Suite 200
New London, CT 06320
(860) 437-3012 or (800) 321-0411
www.twentythirdpublications.com

Photos: @stock.adobe.com

ISBN: 978-1-62785-699-7
Printed in the U.S.A.

 A division of Bayard, Inc.

Contents

Dedication

To my husband, children, and grandson—my life is filled with joy because of you.

Thank you, Rob, for making a family with me, for loving me the way you do, for strengthening me, for laughing with me, for the excitement of the next adventure and the promise of "never a dull moment" even before "I do." I wouldn't want to do this with anyone but you.

Thank you, Kelsey (and Mike), Ryan (and Katie), and Maddie, for helping me to know the joy of motherhood, for teaching me about life, love, prayer, faith, and God, in ways only a child can teach a parent. I am so proud of each of you. I did not know what unconditional love was until I loved you. I couldn't imagine how much my heart could expand until I loved you. You show me what is possible.

And to our little Liam, my first grandchild: Oh, the pure joy my heart feels as I hold you in my arms and you look up at me! This must be how God loves us.

INTRODUCTION

The need to reimagine faith formation took on a whole new urgency in 2020 due to a global pandemic. Church leaders quickly moved to employ new technology, reformat delivery methods, and develop ways in which catechetical leaders could gather children and their families digitally. Many parishes closed their doors to visitors due to COVID restrictions. Liturgies became virtual, hosted on Livestream and Facebook Live or recorded and posted on parish websites. When churches could open, it was to 25 percent capacity, then 50 percent. Many took reservations for mass, offered guidance for socially distanced practices, and explained new policies for receiving the Eucharist. A new vocabulary entered our communications: unprecedented, Zoom, pivoted, hybrid faith formation, home-allied approaches. We navigated so many unknowns in a landscape that just kept changing. Pastors, ministry leaders, and the families they serve were living in a new world that sometimes seemed unrecognizable.

There was much suffering, from the loss of lives to the loss of work, the loss of in-person school for many children, and an experience of incredible isolation for much of our population. Families juggled the responsibilities of work, raising and teaching their children, and caring for aging parents, all from within their own homes. Our immediate worlds became smaller as we existed under stay-at-home orders, and yet, we also began to realize how interconnected we are as a human family—how our own actions, big and small, impact those around us, both near and far.

There were blessings amid the suffering as well. Families rediscovered quality time spent together over meals and at leisure. Sabbath took on new significance as families discovered what it really means to be the domestic church. Catechetical leaders equipped and empowered parents to lead prayer and have faith conversations with their children at home. Parents created prayer spaces at home and answered questions about the mass as families watched on televisions, computers, and iPads. Families celebrated holy days and seasons at home, making wreaths for Advent, tracing the sign of the cross on each other's foreheads with ashes at the start of Lent, and washing each other's feet on Holy Thursday. One mom shared her excitement with me as she explained that her family was creating new traditions and experiencing the mass in such new ways. Like so many other parents, she was used to "shushing" the kids at mass, missing more of the homily than not, worrying about what the people in the pews in front of and behind her were thinking as one child tried to crawl under the pew and another pinched his sister, and the youngest cried that she had to go to the bathroom. She said this time spent worshipping at home helped them learn so much but also made them appreciate what they were missing. She looked forward to returning to church because she had a newfound appreciation for the beauty of the mass, for the community that she longed to be a part of once again. She couldn't wait to join others in song and participate in the elements of the liturgy that could not be re-created at home.

Coming out of the pandemic, we have an incredible opportunity to connect the home church (the domestic church) and the church of the community (the parish). How can we honor the experience families have had over these many months while inviting them back to the parish? How can we affirm the experience they've had and not dismiss it as we rush to get back to "normal"? I believe those parishes that do this well will build thriving communities moving forward. We must honor and lift up the home church that families created through prayer, faith practices, faith conversations, and sacrifice. If we unpack this experience together, connect it back to the teachings of our faith, to the local faith community, to liturgy, create the space to listen to families, to hear their individual and shared experiences (the "joys and the hopes, the griefs and the anxieties," as Vatican II put it), the Church will be renewed. I am convinced of this, and it is to this end that I wrote this book.

I offer it as a message of hope and encouragement to pastors, deacons, faith formation directors, youth ministers, and other ministry leaders, and as a guide for reimagining faith formation for today's Church. I'll share insights from experience, research, and Church documents. We'll explore the guiding principles that will help you make those first steps or affirm the steps you've already taken. Using those essential building blocks, I'll present strategies and tips for designing and implementing an approach to faith formation that puts families first. If you're already offering a family approach, I'll give you tools for evaluating and adapting your model, confronting resistance, and building an entire network of faith formators in your community. There are questions at the end of each chapter (or each lesson, in chapter 2) for you to use with your team as you reflect on the next best step for your parish.

Why should you read this book? I have worked in the area of family faith formation for almost twenty years: first as a parish leader, then in a diocesan role, and eventually as a presenter, trainer, consultant, and coach. I will share what I learned in the early days of navigating this paradigm shift in a parish, the mistakes we made, and the quick wins we celebrated, and I will share the experience of communities across the country—stories from parishes that have offered some form of family faith formation for ten, fifteen, even twenty-five years. In working with these leaders, I have discovered that there is not one way to do this. One size does not fit all. It is an approach, not a program. It is a theological understanding of who families are and who we are called to be as Church today. I walk leaders through the steps of discerning the answer to questions like: What is our vision? Where do we start?

What are our next steps? This is not my story; it is the story of pastors and catechetical leaders who have walked with families in a manner that invites them into belonging and believing. It is the story of families who have shared their experiences of transformation, of falling in love with Jesus and his Church again or for the first time.

In 2020, pastors and catechetical leaders felt they had permission to let go of systems and structures that were no longer working; out of necessity, they began to embrace new models, new strategies, new technology. At the same time, toward the end of the shutdown, many felt incredible pressure to return to "normal," going back to "how we've always done it." I hope the lessons shared—the methods, strategies, and design tips offered in this book—equip you to resist that temptation. I pray this offers you hope, allows you to give yourself permission to experiment, and inspires you to imagine new ways to engage every family in your faith community.

In *Let Us Dream*, Pope Francis defines this as a "clarifying moment" and calls us to not let it pass us by. My hope from this strange time is that a renewed Church emerges, built of local communities of disciples, families living the Gospel, and people sharing faith.

PART ONE

An Integrated Approach to Faith Formation

The family is a proclamation of faith in that it is the natural place in which faith can be lived in a simple and spontaneous manner.

It "has a unique privilege: transmitting the Gospel by rooting it in the context of profound human values. On this human base, Christian initiation is more profound: the awakening of the sense of God; the first steps in prayer; education of the moral conscience; formation in the Christian sense of human love, understood as a reflection of the love of God the Father, the Creator. It is, indeed, a Christian education more witnessed to than taught, more occasional than systematic, more ongoing and daily than structured into periods."

DIRECTORY FOR CATECHESIS, #227

ONE

Order Disrupted

My family moved to a small town in the Midwest when I was eleven years old. It was a tight-knit farming community full of families whose surnames were Fitzgerald, Doyle, Gallagher, Delaney, or started with Mc or O'. Though I had been baptized Catholic, my formation had been somewhat limited up to that point. When one of my new classmates asked me to go to CCD (Confraternity of Christian Doctrine) with her one Monday night, I said yes. Almost everyone I'd met in this little town went to St. Joseph's Catholic Church on Monday nights. I was curious.

My first visit went largely unnoticed by anyone except my classmates. During the second, the teacher asked me a few questions. By the third visit, I received an invitation from the pastor to come to his office. Fr. Ed Joyce wanted to know what had brought me to class these past few weeks. I was obviously new to town, so he asked, "Is your family Catholic?" He wanted to know if my parents intended to join the parish or enroll me in classes. Soon I was on the phone with my parents, handing the receiver over to Fr. Joyce. Before long, he was at our house for dinner, and soon after that, we became parishioners.

Though I received minimal formal faith formation before this time (only Sunday School until I was six years old) and didn't make my First Communion with a class of peers at age seven or wear the beautiful white dress many young girls wear on that important occasion—I am grateful for the faith formation I received at home. I am thankful for the witness of faith my parents gave me, for the "simple and spontaneous manner" in which the Catholic faith was passed down to me. I learned about love and sacrifice, forgiveness and mercy, in everyday family life. I learned prayers and Bible stories at bedtime. I learned wonder and awe on our walks, and in the backyard, and in every moment of learning about the world.

My formal Catholic education was delayed in the late 1960s/early 1970s as my father wrestled with the changes that came after the Second Vatican Council (1962–1965). But even in that, I learned what it looked like to sit with the questions, to struggle in search for answers. My parents gave me many gifts of faith practice, encouraged me in faith conversation at home, sent me to Providence Catholic High School, and were there for my graduation from Catholic Theological Union just a few years ago.

"Faith is not a linear process" (*Directory for Catechesis*, #224), and thus we are all on our own journey. My father's journey was not a straight line; it had starts and stops along the way. His path would greatly influence his children's paths as well. Our move to a small Irish Catholic town would be a catalyst in my own faith life, as I was immersed in a community that was rich in Catholic identity. I celebrated my First Communion at St. Joe's and was confirmed there. My husband Rob and I were married there. Fr. Ed O'Malley baptized our children there. It was the first place I would volunteer as a catechist: when I was right out of high school and years later, when I registered my children for religious education.

When my children entered those religious education classrooms, very little had changed since I went to CCD. The classrooms looked the same. The hallways looked the same. Children came to class for one hour or so a week, about thirty weeks out of the year. The catechists read from books published for the specific purpose of forming children in the faith. Children would learn prayers, Catholic vocabulary, and Church doctrine. They would prepare to receive sacraments. This was the order of things. This was the way young Catholics were learning about their faith in classrooms across the country. We knew how to do this. Pastors and parish leaders asked for volunteers who became catechists. Catechetical leaders ran the programs and trained catechists. Catechists taught children. Leaders would tell me later, "We've always done it this way."

The world around us was changing dramatically, though. It no longer supported this model of faith formation the way it had in past decades. My little town was no longer primarily Catholic (or Irish). Parishes no longer functioned as the social epicenter of the community. A maintenance model based on what worked then doesn't work in today's culture. Catholics are walking away from the faith and not returning when they get married or have children, as had been expected in past generations. It's time to reimagine faith formation.

If you've been reading the signs of the times, you already know this. In 2014, the Pew Forum on Religion and Public Life published its research titled *America's Changing Religious Landscape*, reporting that "Of all the major denominations, Catholicism has experienced the greatest net losses as a result of affiliation changes." The study further revealed that 35 percent of the Millennial generation claimed no religious affiliation. Called the "Nones" (because when asked about their religious identity, they answer "none"), this group was (and is) growing faster than any other religious category.

The news was especially alarming for those dedicated to the faith formation of our youth. Young people are "going, going, gone," says author Robert McCarty. McCarty summarized the results of research done by St. Mary's Press in collaboration with the Center for Applied Research in the Apostolate (CARA) in the book *Going, Going, Gone*. CARA studied the dynamics of "disaffiliated young Catholics" and the mass exodus of young people after receiving the sacrament of Confirmation. The drop-off religious education model of past generations (where parents dropped off their kids and picked them up an hour later) is not accomplishing the goal of forming young people in the faith. If we are called to "go and make disciples" (Matthew 28:19–20), at some point we have to ask ourselves why we keep doing what we're doing when we know it isn't accomplishing that goal. The pandemic accelerated this crisis. And yet, this is also why I see our current situation as an opportunity.

The call for the new evangelization has been defined as outreach to baptized Catholics who have become distant from the faith, and it emboldens us to do more to reach the people in our own pews.

Sherry Weddell's *Forming Intentional Disciples: The Path to Knowing and Following Jesus* was a wake-up call for many ministers. In 2012, Weddell emphasized the existence of people in our churches on Sunday morning who have never had an encounter with the person of Christ, though they identify as Catholic. Weddell cited research that relayed the growth of the religiously unaffiliated. The percentage of the unaffiliated is higher among the young. One study reported more distressing news: that 68 percent of those families who identify as Catholic do not have their children in either Catholic schools, religious education, faith formation programs, or youth ministry (CARA, 2015). If we are to reach young people and their families, we must rethink our methods of formation and evangelization.

The most recent research outlines even more dire statistics:

- 26.1 million Americans who were baptized Catholic are no longer practicing (*Outreach to the Unaffiliated*, USCCB)
- 26 percent of the U.S. adult population identify as unaffiliated (*Outreach to the Unaffiliated*, USCCB)
- 79 percent of those disaffiliated from religion before the age of twenty-four (*Outreach to the Unaffiliated*, USCCB)
- Americans' membership in houses of worship continued to decline last year, dropping below 50 percent for the first time in Gallup's eight-decade trend
- In 2020, 47 percent of Americans said they belonged to a church, synagogue, or mosque, down from 50 percent in 2018 and 70 percent in 1999 (Gallup)

I first began to follow this research as a youth minister in the early 2000s, when I heard about the work of Dr. Christian Smith and the National Study on Youth and Religion. Some of the early research was published in *Soul Searching: The Religious and Spiritual Lives of American Teenagers* in 2005, which Smith wrote with Melinda Lundquist Denton. One thing that surfaced, and that would play out again and again, was the significance of parents' influence on the spiritual lives of their teens. Smith and Lundquist Denton said that parents matter most: "Most American teens turn out religiously to look a lot like their parents....It appears that the relative religious laxity of most U.S. Catholic teenagers significantly reflects the relative religious laxity of their parents." As an educator, minister, and parent, this fascinated me. I knew that however we might reimagine faith formation (and youth ministry), it would have to engage and support the parents *as well as* their children.

All of this research gave reason for us to imagine new models of faith formation almost twenty years ago. Some ministry and thought leaders would do just that. The Diocese of Joliet offered training provided by John Roberto, then from the Center for Ministry Development, now of Lifelong Faith Associates. Roberto helped us imagine what lifelong faith formation might look like: intergenerational and focused on faith conversations, faith practices, gathering, sending. I was convinced of the need to engage parents. Our parish would undergo training from 2004 to 2007, making the shift to a family-centered faith formation approach in 2007. Still, in the years that followed, the majority of Catholic parishes continued to offer drop-off classes, with few to no interactions with parents. That is, until March 2020.

DISRUPTION

I remember getting the word on March 13, 2020, that the Archdiocese of Chicago had released a statement:

> Based on current guidelines from local public health departments, which recommend the cancellation of public gatherings involving 250 or more people, Cardinal Blase J. Cupich, archbishop of Chicago, mandated the suspension until further notice of all liturgical services effective Saturday evening with the regularly scheduled weekend services. In addition, he has mandated the closing of schools operated by the archdiocese, and to close the Pastoral Center and related agency offices until further notice.

Church was closed. Faith formation programs were shut down. Soon after, the governor of the State of Illinois issued a "Stay at Home" order effective at 5 PM on Saturday, March 21, to help contain the spread of the COVID-19 virus.

It felt like the world had stopped. Restaurants were closed. Schools were closed. Everything was put on hold: travel, weddings, baptisms, First Communions, confirmations. The school closures and faith formation disruptions were extensive for some. For many months, in many places, families were stuck at home. Parents worked from home, took care of their children, and, in some cases, looked after aging parents as well. Parents taught their children or helped them learn how to attend virtual classrooms and held homework sessions at night. In addition, if their parish offered programming or assistance, parents taught their children the faith. In other places, school and faith formation became a start/stop process, open when allowed and closed when necessary due to spikes in the virus.

All of my parish, diocesan, and conference travels were canceled during this time. Most events went virtual immediately. I gave a series of webinars for diocesan and parish leaders focused on planning for hybrid or integrated faith formation approaches for 2020–2021 and then again the following year for 2021–2022. I began teaching online master classes on family faith formation for Vibrant Faith. I spoke to more faith formation leaders than I ever had before about empowering and equipping parents in those early months of the pandemic. I witnessed incredible adaptive leadership with leaders who were responsive and flexible. I witnessed creativity born of necessity. This pandemic caused us to enter into a liminal space that would offer a moment to reflect on emerging questions: What's working? What's not? What do we keep? What do we let go of? How do we move forward?

LIMINAL SPACE

Though it was probably not a household word before the pandemic, "liminal" would become a word I would hear over and over throughout this time. My husband and I embraced our empty nester stage of life in recent years, so liminal space was something with which I was familiar. I attended the STORY conference in 2019. The theme that year was "Between the No Longer and Not Yet." It was one of the most inspiring conferences I've attended, as presenters shared stories of grief, pain, redemption, and triumph over difficult challenges. It seems liminal space provides an occasion for incredible growth when we're open to it. We have experienced many individual and collective losses throughout this time of pandemic. I don't want to diminish that in any way. It is real. But we are also offered this opportunity to grow, to be made new again.

Richard Rohr, OFM, describes liminal space as being "betwixt and between the familiar and the completely unknown." It is that space where we know more about where we've been than about where we're going. Rohr says that in this space, we need to *not* do things "according to our usual successful patterns" but instead should be willing to try and fail, to experiment, to find creative approaches. He says, "It would be difficult to exist in this time of global crisis and not feel caught between at least two worlds—the one we knew and the one to come. Our consciousness and that of future generations has been changed."

Rohr speaks of this kind of rhythm as the wisdom pattern: order, disorder, reorder. When we experience order, everything is fine, in its place. We maintain the status quo. Then some disruption occurs that throws it all into chaos: disorder. When this happens, we are called to reorder, to create again, to be co-creators with the Holy Spirit. It is the age-old story of our faith: life, death, and resurrection. This liminal space is the waiting of Holy Saturday when we cannot know what comes next, but we wait with anticipation, and perhaps some trepidation, in the promise of new life.

This pause allows us to pay attention to emerging questions so that we might find new pathways, a new normal, or at least a "next normal." Though we might feel stuck in this messy middle, we are not meant to stay here. In his book *The Land Between: Finding God in Difficult Transitions*, Jeff Manion describes the journey of the Israelites. They are stuck in "the undesired space between more desirable spaces." Some leaders might want to return to what we knew before, but there is no going back. And as Manion notes, "The desert is not intended to be [the Israelites'] final destination but rather a necessary middle space where they will be formed as a people and established in their connection to God." We, too, are being formed as a people, being established in our connection to God and to his Church.

REORDER

As Church leaders, we are experiencing this pain point at the intersection of exhaustion from a difficult two years (or more) and uncertainty or anxiety about what to do next. The questions we ask, the decisions we make, the approaches we try will all influence what reordering looks like. We may not know what comes next, but I believe the parishes that thrive in the future will be those that do not rush past this moment, who listen to their people, who unpack this experience, and who take the experience our families had of their home church (the domestic church) and connect it back to the church of the community (the parish). For some families, this was the first time they were aware of their own domestic church. This was an authentic experience of what it means to be a domestic church. They created prayer spaces at home. They worshipped at home, participating in liturgies via Facebook Live or their parish's Livestream channel. They had to be intentional about all of this. Parents taught their children about the faith and lived it out at home, sometimes in very new ways. We cannot assume that people were not in some way nourished in faith during this time, that they weren't able to grow closer to God, simply because they were not present in the church buildings. Unpacking this and making those connections will require us to listen and to accompany people. Some have experienced isolation, disconnection, disillusionment, depression, despair. Others found a new appreciation for the liturgy, offered prayers of thanksgiving for a new understanding of Sabbath. And still others felt a mix of both. We need to hear the stories and ask people what they need. We need to meet them where they are, even if that's at home—for now.

By innovating in this space, we have the chance to breathe new life into our Church. As we explore these innovations, I'll focus on the methods, curriculum, and resources that leaders curated and created, of course, but I also want us to pay attention to the way Church leaders responded during the pandemic using digital means. And, most important, I want you to see the way storytelling can be used to build community and accompany families. When done well, this practice increases belonging, encourages ownership over one's faith growth, and empowers our people as evangelizers in their faith communities.

Questions for Reflection

1. What gives you hope today?

2. How has the trend of Catholic disaffiliation affected your ministry?

3. Did the pandemic accelerate this reality for you? If so, how?

4. As you look at how you responded during the pandemic, what would you want to keep as you move forward?

5. What does reordering look like for you today?

6. How will you innovate in this liminal space?

7. How has the pandemic caused you to think differently about your ministry?

8. How do you want your ministry to be different in the future? What is your long-term vision of faith formation in your parish?

9. How do we move from just surviving COVID to thriving in our ministries?

10. What resonates in this chapter? What challenges you? Or what would you challenge?

The Church finds herself facing a "new stage of evangelization" because even in this change of era the risen Lord continues to make all things new (cf. Revelation 21:5)....The ecclesial journey itself is marked by difficulties and by the need for spiritual, moral, and pastoral renewal. And yet the Holy Spirit continues to arouse the thirst for God within people, and within the Church a new fervor, new methods, and new expressions for the proclamation of the good news of Jesus Christ.

DIRECTORY FOR CATECHESIS, #38

TWO

Innovation and Transformation: Lessons from a Pandemic

Most of us were ready to say goodbye to 2020 by the end of that year, but it's important to review the lessons we learned from those first pandemic months, starting with moving liturgy online and then looking at the varied ways we partnered with parents. We've known for a long time the benefits of partnering with parents, but nothing before this pandemic led to such widespread efforts to explore home-allied approaches.

Here are just a few of the lessons we learned from the strategies employed and experiments launched by responsive and innovative church leaders in 2020:

1. Use technology to reach people, to offer people an experience of God, an opportunity to participate in the liturgy, and a way to feel belonging in the faith community.

2. Use digital tools and methods to deliver faith formation content to children, youth, parents, adults, families, and intergenerational groups, such as

    -   videoconferencing apps

- classroom management or learning management system apps
- supplemental learning apps

3. Focus your evangelization and catechetical efforts on the two things that research says have the greatest impact on faith formation: God-talk and faith practices.

4. Connect parents to one another and to the larger faith community.

5. Encourage families to create their own faith formation plan (or a portion of it). Then invite them to share their experiences.

6. Build or strengthen community through storytelling. Be sure to include digital storytelling.

I'll explore each of these strategies further, with the understanding that there may be some overlap across strategies. For example, storytelling could be integrated into each of these lessons, but it is so essential to an integrated faith formation approach, it deserves a section dedicated to this kind of narrative power.

LESSON 1
USE TECHNOLOGY

Use technology to reach people, to offer people an experience of God, an opportunity to participate in the liturgy, and a way to feel belonging in the faith community.

I never imagined a time when we would be unable to gather to celebrate the Eucharist. This made the pandemic real for me. I applaud the bishops, pastors, and the many ministry leaders and staff for how quickly they pivoted. We didn't go without a Sunday celebration. Some small or rural parishes may not have been prepared to make that virtual shift right away, but even then, leaders pointed their parishioners to the archdiocesan or diocesan websites for available online masses and prayers, and some parishioners even tuned in to the pope's celebration of the Eucharist on the Vatican website. Most parishes made some accommodation to offer the mass online immediately. Some had previously offered access to one or more of their weekend masses online for the homebound and others who were unable to be physically present in the community for one reason or another: these parishes were ready. Some share that they have no intention of discontinuing that practice, since it continues to meet an expressed need and has engaged those they were not previously reaching.

The digital world can be an environment rich in humanity; a network not of wires but of people....Christian witness, thanks to the internet, can thereby reach the peripheries of human existence....The Church needs to be... present in the world of communication, in order to dialogue with people today and to help them encounter Christ. ■ *Pope Francis, 48th World Communications Day, January 24, 2014*

There were mixed responses from theologians, liturgists, and pastoral leaders. Parishioners were grateful for the opportunity to honor the Sabbath in this way, grateful to be united with their parish family or to be able to participate in masses all around the world, or with family near and far. Some leaders worried, though, that this might confuse people in the long run, making them think this was "normal." Church leaders provided tips to parishioners on how they could make it special, how they could practice reverence even at home. Others gave suggestions for how a person might practice the Liturgy of the Hours at home, as a gathered prayer service (so it was more participatory and embodied), rather than "watch" the mass on the television. We still have much to learn about people's experience of the liturgy throughout the pandemic, but I have heard incredibly positive stories of how livestreamed masses made the Church present for people at a time when they felt otherwise isolated. Parishioners liked seeing their pastors and other ministers, often the faith formation staff, who helped with the celebration of the liturgy.

My own experience as a parishioner was life-giving. I missed the Eucharist. I missed the community. And my husband and I were ready to return when we were finally able to do so. But during the initial restrictions, we were grateful to celebrate Sundays via Livestream with our parish family. I've reflected for some time on what made me feel connected, supported, and nourished, in an effort to share the answer with other leaders.

Our pastor and his staff encouraged us to participate fully, and they offered suggestions for how we might do that. Fr. Tom Hurley acted as if we were all in the sacred space together, acknowledging every week that some of us were in living rooms, kitchens, or basements but that we came together now around this altar, still together. A staff member facilitated the chat on Livestream, welcoming us all to the liturgy, telling us where we could find the worship aid, inviting us to greet one another in the chat. And people did. People shared their "good morning" messages: "Glad to see you here, Joe," "Praying for you, Mary," "Joining you from Ireland today, friends, with my parents."

The pastor and staff also encouraged us to "watch" with friends, to text each other support, to text each other during the sign of peace, to grab breakfast or brunch together after mass (virtually, of course), and to share our experience on social media using the hashtags #WeareOSP and #StillTogether. The result was an incredible strengthening of community. I got to know parishioners of all ages whom I had never met prior to the pandemic. They shared images on Instagram of their family participating in the liturgy around their television in their family room, around a computer at their kitchen table, or, like one mom, with a baby on her lap and an iPad in her hand. I saw images of parents blessing their children. I saw some of the treasured seniors of our community gathering in their backyard for a "watch party," socially distanced as they sat outside with friends and neighbors. One parishioner shared on Instagram, "My cellphone video doesn't do it any justice, but I will never forget the comfort @oldstpats mass, especially the music, gave me during this time. #WeareOSP, #StillTogether 🙏 ♥." Many others affirmed that message or shared their own.

My husband and I texted with friends before mass as they asked, "Hey, are you in the usual pew?" "Glad you're here. Are the kids with you?" We texted again at the sign of peace. At least ten of us offered each other the sign of peace this way, each and every Sunday. That fortified me in ways I'm still not sure I can express. A few times, we gathered after mass for a virtual brunch. I did not see these friends for almost a year outside of these virtual gatherings. On Easter morning in 2020, thirteen of our friends gathered online for prayer and breakfast after mass. We drank orange juice, coffee, or mimosas and ate pancakes, eggs, or cereal while reflecting on life, death, and our hope in the resurrection during a pandemic. We talked about being connected to each other, our families, our parish, our pastor, and God during this time. Having this experience of Church while we were isolated was a truly transformative experience.

Even though my experience felt transformative, my desire to be together participating in the liturgy, physically receiving the Eucharist, being the embodied Christ as a community was not diminished. If anything, it felt stronger. I know I was not alone in this experience. This is why some Catholic leaders have cautioned us not to be too quick to rush past this period of disruption and instead to recognize that people experienced spiritual nourishment, grew in faith, and perhaps started new faith practices all while praying in their own sacred spaces at home. This is worth exploring.

My friend and colleague at Vibrant Faith, Dr. Nancy Going, Director of Research and Resource Development, says:

> Yes, we need to make decisions about pivoting our ministry's vision and practice, but we need (even more) to give ourselves space and time to drop back and study what has happened and is happening in the lives of the next generation of Christ-followers.... What is happening in the discipling and formation work of churches will rise to the top as a VERY significant thread—perhaps the MOST significant thread—in the ongoing narrative of the impact of the global pandemic on the American Christian church.[1]

She goes on to share the work of another colleague, Dr. Tanya Campen, and her new book, *Holy Work with Children: Making Meaning Together.* Dr. Going says:

> [Campen's] research is prodding us to shift our attention from what WE are doing to focus exclusively on teaching children and young people, to paying attention to what God is doing in their lives and then help THEM to pay attention to how and where they are experiencing God's presence. We need to pay attention to what they are paying attention to—what aspects of God's nature they are naturally drawn to in this season of upheaval.

---

1   https://vibrant-faith-catalyst.mn.co/posts/what-were-learning-learning-to-pay-attention

This is the work of faith formation. This is a different kind of paying attention. This is what I mean when I say we need to unpack the families' experiences of what the Church has been during this time, do some meaning-making work, and connect it back to the experience of being Church *together* in our own faith communities. Where have they experienced God? Where have they found meaning in this experience of the domestic church, of finding God's presence and activity in the midst of this disruption? In that unpacking, we might find ourselves walking with families in new ways, listening to their stories, helping them return to the faith community.

Many Church leaders have expressed their worry that people are not returning, that they may not come back. It's too soon to think this is an end result of COVID. Cardinal Joseph W. Tobin said in his February 2021 pastoral letter to the Archdiocese of Newark, "Returning to Grace: A Pastoral Letter on the Eucharist":

> As I'm sure you are aware, declining Mass attendance was a serious concern long before the pandemic. Has the current crisis accelerated this trend, or have we grown in our appreciation for the Eucharist precisely because we were denied access to it for so long? Has absence made our hearts grow fonder?…Until that day [that we can all return safely] we must allow the Holy Spirit to guide us in helping those who cannot receive the Eucharist to encounter the person of Jesus in personal prayer, Scripture and in service to God's people.

Cardinal Tobin believes we will look back on this time as the "Great Eucharistic Fast," that it will increase our desire for the Eucharist and for our communities, but that we will need to be patient with people in our efforts to bring them back. We will need to accompany them. I am reminded here of Jesus' words and actions on the road to Emmaus (Luke 24:13–25). He joined the two disciples on the road. He asked them questions and *listened* to their responses. He heard them express their disillusionment, their despair. "We *were* hoping that he would be the one to redeem Israel," they said, with eyes downcast. Jesus walked with them and let them share their experiences, their feelings, even their despair, and *then* he began to unpack Scripture and help make sense of all they carried with them.

The next part is just as crucial to understanding how this might reframe our conversations about this pandemic time, and our need to have these conversations, in the future. They recognize Jesus in the breaking of the bread. That was revelation! But I think they found the real meaning-making as they discussed their "burning hearts" and returned to Jerusalem to share their story, as they unpacked their experience together all the way back and with the disciples when they got there. The meaning is not always found in the moment of revelation but in the telling of that revelation, the sharing and processing of the transformation that is happening with us, within our own "burning hearts."

In the story of the road to Emmaus, we find a model for the ministry of accompaniment:

- Ask questions.
- Listen.
- Tell stories.
- Walk with one another.
- Share your blessings and your brokenness with one another.

We must give space for people to share their experiences. I know people who had not been to mass regularly in quite some time, but during COVID, when the mass was virtual, they participated in the liturgy every Sunday. Old St. Pat's, my home parish, had at least four times as many devices tune into the livestreamed Sunday mass than could fit into our church. Many devices probably counted for more than one person participating in a household. Surely this tells us that people were open to the Church and our liturgy in new ways. People have many reasons for being away from the Church. Some have disaffiliated because of some harm or pain they experienced in a parish;

others because of a lack of trust of institutions, including, or even especially, the Church. For some it's a deep grief: the loss of a spouse or other loved one, divorce, or some other kind of suffering. And for still others it is just a drifting away or even indifference. Could this be an opportunity to grow in relationship with them, to rebuild trust, to help them heal from their loss, their grief or pain, to walk with them in whatever they are going through now? I believe it is.

The Archdiocese of Chicago offered advice to this end in its Summer 2021 Resource Guide.[2] They asked leaders to focus on "fulfilling the mission, not on filling their spaces." They suggested that finding ways to bless people where they were might be more important than getting them to show up "where we are." They reminded leaders that there may be some reentry anxiety. They asked leaders to be pastoral, to not criticize people when they aren't yet ready to return. Just stay in the conversation. Ask them questions. Listen. They suggested to priests and deacons that their homilies should be a source of hope and healing. Hybrid options of online and in-person liturgy will be with us for a while, they said, and we must embrace the technology of livestreaming. Finally, they said, what we are now experiencing is likely not a new normal but a "next normal." We may continue to face unanticipated disruptions, so we must be patient, flexible, and ready to adapt.

What does this have to do with faith formation? Everything! We have separated faith formation from the liturgy for too long. We complain that families bring their children for faith formation, or for sacrament preparation, but we don't see them at mass. If we don't try to rush back to "normal," if we offer families a holistic and integrated approach to faith formation that is focused on the liturgy, the community, the passing on of faith, and the living into our faith, if we continue to use the tools and methods we discovered during this disruption, I believe we will have stronger faith formation programs and more vibrant parishes. We will see families living and growing in their faith.

---

2   https://pvm.archchicago.org/documents/87254/88701/Restore+Illinois+Phase+5+Resource+Guide_v2.pdf/29012498-a08b-44d0-afa7-2045416f8ab8

An integrated approach includes liturgy. Parishes might want to consider a lectionary-based approach, using curriculums, like Pflaum's *Gospel Weeklies*, that support this approach to faith formation. Pflaum's supporting resources include materials for gathering rituals, seasonal celebrations, outlines for drive-through events, and more. Even if a parish does not choose a lectionary-based model, a multi-component or integrated approach can include a focus on the celebration of the liturgy, on learning the faith in a way that is connected to liturgy.

The *Directory for Catechesis* (2020) directs us to see the liturgy as one of the "essential and indispensable sources of the Church's catechesis" because "the two belong to one another in the very act of believing."

> Although each has its own specificity, the liturgy and catechesis, understood in the light of the Church's tradition, are not to be juxtaposed but rather to be seen in the context of the Christian and ecclesial life as both being oriented toward bringing to life the experience of God's love....The liturgy is "the privileged place for catechizing the People of God." This is not to be understood in the sense that the liturgy should lose its celebratory character and be turned into catechesis, or that catechesis is superfluous. Although it is correct that the two contributions should maintain their specificity, it must be recognized that the liturgy is the summit and source of the Christian life....Catechesis is intrinsically linked with the whole of liturgical and sacramental activity, for it is in the sacraments, especially in the Eucharist, that Christ Jesus works in fullness for the transformation of human beings. (*Directory for Catechesis*, #95)

An integrated approach to faith formation includes liturgy because "liturgy and catechesis are inseparable and nourish one another" (*Directory for Catechesis*, #96).

Questions for Reflection

1. How or where do you include liturgical catechesis in your ministry?

2. What connections have you made between the domestic church and the parish?

3. How might you strengthen these connections?

4. How did your parishioners experience community during the pandemic? How might you strengthen the sense of community? The sense of belonging?

5. How do you believe this "Great Eucharistic Fast" will impact the Church?

6. Will your parish continue to "broadcast" the liturgy online? How will you welcome people back in person while walking with people who are not yet ready to return?

7. Dr. Tanya Campen suggests that we are called to pay attention to what God is doing in children's lives and "help THEM to pay attention to how and where they are experiencing God's presence"... to pay attention to the ways they are naturally drawn to God. What could that look like in your ministry?

8. Dr. Nancy Going suggests that we need to "give ourselves space and time to drop back and study what has happened and is happening in the lives of the next generation of Christ-followers... what is happening in the discipling and formation work of churches." How will you and your parish leaders "drop back and study" what is happening? How can you plan that space and study intentionally?

9. What was your experience of Church during the pandemic? How do you continue to nourish yourself spiritually? Communally?

10. What resonates in this exploration of lesson 1? What challenges you? Or what would you challenge?

LESSON 2
USE DIGITAL TOOLS AND METHODS

Use digital tools and methods to deliver faith formation content to children, youth, parents, adults, families, and intergenerational groups.

During the pandemic restrictions, ministry leaders added a wide variety of digital tools to their catechetical toolbox. Most of these applications can be categorized as one of three types of tools: videoconferencing apps, like Zoom, Skype, Google Meet, or Facebook Messenger; classroom (or learning) management system apps, like Google Classroom, Edmodo, Flipgrid, or Neo; and finally, supplemental learning apps, like Edpuzzle, Khan Academy, Kahoot!, Padlet, or Quizlet. Through the use of these tools, leaders delivered faith formation content and conversations in wholly new ways. Many leaders developed digital faith hubs or created digital playlists that allowed families to pick and choose flexible ways to nurture the faith of their children. Here we'll review just a few of those tools.

VIDEOCONFERENCING APPS
When it came to videoconferencing apps, Zoom was probably the most utilized tool across the Church: for children's classes, youth ministry programs, adult faith formation, family faith formation, and other

The web and social networks...provide an extraordinary opportunity for dialogue, encounter and exchange between persons, as well as access to information and knowledge. ■ *Pope Francis,* **Christus Vivit,** *#87* ministry meetings. Though some have said that they experienced "Zoom fatigue," the benefits of using this platform far outweighed the challenges. First, when we could not gather physically, we had a way we could deliver content personally. We had a means to still meet with our people. Zoom was used not just for classes, but for diocesan and parish staff meetings, small group gatherings, prayer services, and, in a few cases, even for liturgy.

This was not without its challenges. Holding classes on Zoom could be difficult, especially in the beginning, when it was all so new. Children can be hard to engage on a screen, so many parishes moved to children-and-parent virtual gatherings. Leaders still had to work hard to find ways to engage families across all ages. It forced leaders, teachers, and catechists to be creative. I spoke with leaders who gathered regularly with parents or with families as they moved faith formation completely online. We explored their answers to these questions: What will you keep as you move forward? What do you need to let go of?

One parish met regularly with parents to check in, to see how they were doing, and to facilitate a conversation on the lessons that parents would lead at home. The director said she felt that the most important part of this process was the check-in. Parents connected with one another. She wrapped this in prayer where parents contributed their intentions. She said some days it was heart-wrenching. Not every parent participated at this level. Some resisted, but even then, she reached out, made phone calls, listened to what was going on in the family, what was keeping families away: schedules, hardships, and more. This practice greatly impacted her ministry, and I believe it impacted those families and their relationship with the Church as well. The personal check-in approach is something she will continue.

Many parishes held children's classes via Zoom. Catechists struggled in some cases, but soon they learned tricks about sharing their screen, allowing chat with the whole group or only with the host (not students one-on-one with each other), arranging breakout rooms so they had an adult in the space to facilitate. Everyone became more efficient at using the technology. It wasn't the same as being in person, but there were benefits. Diocesan offices ran webinars on how to use the technology. Catholic websites like Strong Catholic Family Faith (catholicfamilyfaith.org) curated how-to videos. Through all of this, we learned some best practices. For example:

- Record sessions and provide a link for viewing for those who are unable to make the learning session or gathering.
- Emphasize the use of the chat during live sessions so that even those who are more introverted can participate in the conversations.
- Use other tools that are easily integrated with Zoom, like polling or adding a link to a Google Forms project in the chat to insert a collaborative activity or feature in the session.

I was facilitating a virtual focus group for a parish in New Jersey in 2020 when a woman we'll call Evelyn (because we promised participants' privacy) said she wanted to share her experience of using Zoom. Evelyn was in her late 70s, had no previous experience with Zoom, and knew people thought she would be resistant. Her response was quite the opposite. She was open and excited to learn to use this technology. She used to belong to a small Christian community—a Bible study group that had been together for years. They slowly grew into more of a faith-sharing group who studied the Bible. She said, "It was such a gift, these women. They meant everything to me." But she described how slowly, through the years, as people retired and moved away, or as people got older and were no longer as mobile as they used to be, her group got smaller. She had stopped attending regularly when she stopped driving. Then COVID changed that. Her small group began meeting online, using Zoom. All of a sudden, she didn't have to leave the house. She called friends who had retired to warmer climates. Evelyn said it was like a homecoming, a reunion of good friends near and far. She described it as a lifeline during this crisis. Instead of isolation, she experienced community—a community she had missed intensely prior to the pandemic.

Others in the focus group contributed to the conversation. A mother of four children said she never takes part in parish events because childcare is an issue. With events and groups moving online, she had the opportunity to participate because the children could be in other rooms, and at some point during the evening event, her husband would arrive to handle the bedtime routine. She loved being able to participate in a MOMS (Ministry of Mothers Sharing) group that connected her with other moms. She was enjoying learning about Catholic Social Teaching with the Peace and Social Justice ministry at a time when civil unrest affected her community. It seemed relevant to her life, and she felt connected. This helped her discern how she might be called to respond in faith.

These are but a few of the reasons we need to continue using the technology that we were forced to turn to during the pandemic. It opened up possibilities for homebound folks that were life-giving. Small-group leaders shared that people who were quiet before seemed to come out of their shells. I heard again and again that it was *more* intimate, in some ways. Not everyone will choose the Zoom option for a faith formation offering, but for those who would otherwise not participate, we have new pathways for reaching them. We might even want to offer multiple delivery methods for the same learning event or microlearning sessions across varying platforms.

Many parishes ran sacrament preparation retreats on Zoom. The parent and child could sit around the screen to hear the lesson, then turn to each other (with microphones muted) for conversation or practice. Confirmands and their sponsors did the same; sponsors who could not participate during in-person retreats prior to the pandemic due to geographical issues were no longer excluded. Now they had the opportunity to be a part of the preparation process in a real way.

We've grown accustomed to this technology, so perhaps it's time to imagine all the ways we might use this tool in the future. How can we engage families in our parishes' ministries in person or from home? How might we reach parishioners who have walked away?

CLASSROOM MANAGEMENT APPS

It wasn't just Zoom that changed the way we ministered during the pandemic. One of the most exciting developments for a teacher like me was the incredibly inventive educational tools that were available to use—and often were free for educators. Google Classroom, Flipgrid, Edmodo, Kahoot!, and Quizlet all helped leaders, teachers, and catechists to create unique learning experiences for children and their families. Some programs were even integrated by publishers for easy use with their textbooks. Our Sunday Visitor integrated Flipgrid with their *Alive in Christ* (AIC) series online. They created step-by-step guides for leaders detailing how they could personalize their lessons and manage their gathered or virtual classroom using this tool. The publishers created simple how-to videos for leaders and parents. Parish leaders became curators and creators of lesson activities that could enhance the text's materials.

A parish that used the AIC curriculum could curate or create videos for their lessons. Take, for example, the Grade 2 chapter, which teaches the young person about prayer: it includes the Lord's Prayer, five basic forms of prayer, how prayer is important to our relationship with God, and how sacramentals might assist us in prayer. One parish used the curated videos provided by the publisher: one on the Lord's Prayer and a second one on the crucifix. Another parish created a video in their worship space, recording their pastor teaching about the Lord's Prayer. They also recorded a video with parish leaders sharing their personal sacramentals that enhance their own prayer lives. Both options serve the lesson. This chapter of the Grade 2 AIC resource asks the learner:

- How can you talk to God?
- Share a prayer you wrote or one you like to pray.

Learners used the app to record a video of themselves answering those questions. Some parishes asked for video of the learner. Others asked for video of the family completing the task. Leaders shared how moving it was to view the videos recorded by young people and families. They got to know their families more intimately through this process. They got a better idea of how the child or family understood the lesson, compared to just completing a chapter review. It's not that the review should be skipped, or that it is not helpful in checking for understanding. But hearing a child in their own words provides a personal perspective.

Many parishes relied on Google's free tools: Google Classroom, Google Drive, Google Slides, and Google Forms. These could be integrated with other applications as well. Links could be shared in Zoom chats for breakouts, too. Google Classrooms could be used as a classroom management system. Google Drive could be used as a way to house resources, lessons, newsletters, expectations, or other information for parents and young people. A leader could create as many folders as were needed and share the drive or individual folders via a link or invitation.

Google Slides were used in very creative ways. I loved seeing the Google Slides that became a themed lesson. Sometimes catechists or catechetical leaders even included their Bitmoji (a kind of personalized avatar) in the classroom. I've seen Advent-themed slides and Lenten-themed slides. I've seen Catholic Social Teaching slides and anti-racism slides that could be used when facilitating dialogue around some of the seven themes of Catholic Social Teaching. Each image in the slide can link to something outside the slide.

For example, the Advent slide might have an image of a family's living room. In the room we might find a nativity set. It might link to the history of the nativity scene, or to Scripture verses from Luke and Matthew. It could link to Busted Halo's video *Advent in Two Minutes*. It might link to lessons about Mary and Joseph. There might also be an Advent wreath on a table. That could link to a video showing how to make an Advent wreath. It could also link to how we pray with the Advent wreath. One slide could contain many lessons. The possibilities are endless. The slide can be a simple lesson, or multiple lessons across a textbook unit, or a family playlist for a session or a season.

Imagine a slide that shows a church (maybe even your own church): the worship space, the altar, the tabernacle, the ciborium, and the chalice. It might also include the crucifix and the Stations of the Cross. It could include items the priest wears when he celebrates the mass. You could curate or create videos and resources that describe each item. The resources might teach about the mass, or about prayer, such as adoration. Many parishes shared "Kids Liturgy with Miss Heidi"[3] so families could prepare for mass or prepare for their Sunday celebration of the mass at home. To personalize these Google Slides, a leader could link to videos of families or young people saying prayers, singing a hymn, praying the stations, or expressing their devotion to the Eucharist. As you make storytellers of the families in the program, they become the evangelizers in your community. This is just one way to do that.

Katie Bogner, author of *Through the Year with Jesus* and *Through the Year with Mary*, is a catechetical leader in Central Illinois. She created Google Slides for the classes she teaches and provided these editable Google Slides on her website (Looktohimandberadiant.com). The extensive list of lessons includes seasonal lessons, like Advent and Lent; lessons focused on saints, prayer, and sacraments; even a Catholic "Would You Rather?" game. Slides are provided for viewing, and Katie offers instructions for copying and editing, should a leader want to personalize a lesson.

Finally, Google Forms were used in a variety of ways: as registration forms, surveys, or polls linked in a Zoom class, or as a way to capture lessons, or for families' reflections on activities they participated in at home, again sharing their stories in words or images. Google tools became very popular during the pandemic.

SUPPLEMENTAL LEARNING APPS

Leaders and their catechists also used supplemental learning apps, like Kahoot!, Edpuzzle, or Khan Academy. Kahoot! is a learning platform that makes it easy for any individual or group to create, share, and play

---

3   https://www.youtube.com/channel/UCfg9euOFfmsu-xX7S2tCcNA

learning games. Kahoot! games can be played anywhere, in person or virtually, using any device with an internet connection. Leaders and catechists might find prepared content relevant in the art, cultural studies, or social-emotional learning sections. For example, a Día De Los Muertos Trivia game can be found under Culture and Traditions. The Disney game is designed to help the players learn more about the Mexican tradition of the Day of the Dead. It uses the Disney animated film *Coco* to explore the tradition.

Khan Academy was founded by Salman Khan. His dream was to provide a free world-class education to anyone, anywhere. This became their mission. This tool can provide supplemental learning in any number of areas. Studying Rome? Perhaps Judaism in art? Or Christianity in art? There's even a course called Architecture and Liturgy.

VIRTUAL REALITY

One supplemental learning device offers interesting possibilities if we're open to really thinking outside the box. While exploring supplemental learning apps with some leaders who were focused on providing their parishioners with unique learning experiences, we discovered a trend among residential living centers (specifically those designed for seniors and for persons with limited mobility). Some residential living centers are using virtual reality devices for learning, recreation, or therapy to combat social isolation and build community. The learning experiences vary greatly: for example, they offer travel experiences to individuals who are no longer able to travel. They offer individuals with limited mobility an opportunity to experience activities their bodies are no longer able to enjoy: table tennis, swimming, golf, and more.

As one provider of travel programs, National Geographic gives the user an opportunity to swim with the sharks or observe a family of gorillas in their own habitat or learn about cultures and faraway places. Other programs offer visits to a cathedral, to Rome, even to the Vatican. With a little creativity, a leader could offer a virtual field trip to the Holy Land, the Sea of Galilee, or the site of the story of the Good Samaritan. Residential centers then offer weekly gatherings where residents share those experiences. Some emphasize learning new things, while others connect over the nostalgia of activities of the "days of old."

One of the virtual reality (VR) concepts that sparked the most interest was one called "VR for heritage." It is described this way on Oculus' Instagram page:

> When Bear River Band tribal librarian Jessica Cantrell set out to replace inaccurate materials in local school libraries, she realized many of the tribe's cultural histories were fading with aging members. The tribe is now using #VR to capture the oral traditions and sacred spaces that are central to Bear River Band's heritage. With "Bear River, a Nation: What Can Eeling Teach Us?" the tribe's first 360° film (available on YouTube), young tribal members are reconnecting with their culture. "It's important for youth to learn who they are and where they belong in the world," says Cantrell.

This concept led to a discussion about Catholic heritage: the traditions and practices that are often forgotten in some contemporary families. What would it look like to create a VR curriculum that connects young Catholics and their families with the Catholic culture, so those children also "learn who they are and where they belong in the world"? A parish could create its own heritage series using video of its own campus and interviewing the treasured elders in its community. A family could explore beautiful Catholic sites or Catholic prayer experiences. A parish could offer a self-guided retreat that would take place virtually in a beautiful retreat center while the person is actually in their conference room! And there are grants for this technology for learning institutions. Those in tech want to be able to tell good stories: VR for good, VR for education, VR for autism, VR for impact. They tell these stories through hashtags. Might we do the same?

Although it may seem like a reach, much has already been written about virtual reality in the Catholic world. It has been called anti-sacramental and dystopian. Authors have lamented the dangers and the disembodiment. Others, meanwhile, caution us to not dismiss an entire "world" where we have the opportunity to make the Gospel come alive. In an article for the *National Catholic Reporter*, "Virtual Reality and the Coming Catholic Metaverse," author Phyllis Zagano wrote that the Church is changing; virtual church spaces are coming. "It won't be your grandfather's Catholic church. It is not that already."

Questions for Reflection

1. Has the use of Zoom impacted your ministry? Will you continue to use it? If so, what have you learned about using it? How might you use it differently?

2. What technological tool or digital app was most helpful to your ministry these last few years?

3. What technological tool or digital app do you look forward to exploring in the future?

4. How will you use these tools or apps to engage children? Youth? Families? Adults? Our treasured elders in the community?

5. What was the most creative use of technology that you saw in use in ministry this year? Is it something you will adapt for your own setting? If so, how? If not, why?

6. Do you experience curiosity, wonder, or resistance when you think about the use of virtual reality in ministry?

7. What guidelines might you explore to determine when and how you would use videoconferencing apps? Classroom management apps? Supplemental learning apps? VR devices?

8. What resonates in this exploration of lesson 2? What challenges you? Or what would you challenge?

LESSON 3
FOCUS ON GOD-TALK AND FAITH PRACTICES

Focus your evangelization and catechetical efforts on the two things that research says have the greatest impact on faith formation: God-talk and faith practices.

God-talk (faith conversations) and *faith practices* are the two keys to catalyzing faith in young people, according to Search Institute's research. This is where many parish and diocesan leaders excelled from 2020 to 2022. Because most faith communities were unable to gather, ministry leaders provided parents with faith-focused discussion starters. This gave parents an opportunity to have deep and meaningful conversations with their children about matters of faith (and doubt) at a time when that was important for the mental, emotional, and spiritual health of children of all ages.

Church leaders gave parents instructions (and encouragement) for exploring faith themes, prayer, and Scripture at home. For example, leaders shared ideas and lessons for creating a sacred prayer space at home; for praying with their children before meals (or at the end of the day, or in the car); and for sharing Bible stories or facilitating Children's Liturgy of the Word at home. Some leaders even recorded

It is essential that children actually see that, for their parents, prayer is something truly important. Hence moments of family prayer and acts of devotion can be more powerful for evangelization than any catechism class or sermon. ■ *Pope Francis,* **Amoris Laetitia, #288** "story time" videos for families. In many cases, these conversations and practices had a profound impact on parents' confidence as the faith leaders of their family. Parishes didn't just encourage parents, they empowered and equipped them for this role.

DIOCESAN AND ARCHDIOCESAN RESPONSES AND PROJECTS

What did this look like in practice? In the Archdiocese of Atlanta, it looked like *Families Forming Disciples*. The Office of Evangelization and Discipleship created this effort, focused on Jesus' great commission to "go and make disciples" and inspired by Pope Francis' words from *Evangelii Gaudium* about a "missionary option." They described it on their website as "a missionary impulse capable of transforming everything, so that the Church's customs, ways of doing things, times and schedules, language and structures can be suitably channeled for the evangelization of today's world rather than for her self-preservation." Their expressed desire is to create evangelizing parishes and families. The team hopes family members are growing closer to one another and closer to God.

They describe *Families Forming Disciples* as a hybrid family-focused thematic-activity approach where groups of families meet with catechists (in-person or virtually) to encounter the Lord together and to encourage each other to live as the domestic church in and through their home and family life. Their website says they offer this approach "as a specific way to assist parish catechetical leaders, catechists, and parents/families by seeking to engage families in renewed ways, to advance family evangelization and faith formation."

Archbishop Gregory Hartmeyer of Atlanta offers a video welcome to the families, telling them, "The Church and the world need you!" He goes on to say, "We need the faithful witness of families who, in the busyness of ordinary lives, and even in the midst of extraordinary struggles, take time to pray together, have a meal together, and faithfully go to mass together." The diocesan leaders offer training: family faith formation networking and professional development opportunities. This affords parish leaders an opportunity to develop a deeper understanding of families' spiritual, emotional, and practical needs.

I spoke with Patrice Spirou of the Archdiocese of Atlanta about this approach, the lessons, and the feedback they were getting from leaders and parents within their archdiocese and in parishes and diocesan offices throughout the United States and in other countries. She said that in the feedback they receive, families state that they are rediscovering their faith and are praying together more often. "Parish leaders are reporting that many parents, especially fathers, have said that *Families Forming Disciples* has helped them to share their faith with their children in very natural and comfortable ways."

That's the beauty of the program. Parents do not need to be experts; the whole family learns together. Simple and meaningful faith activities are done together as a family. Lessons were provided in their entirety on the website (evangelizationatl.com). PowerPoint slides were provided for each lesson, along with discussion starters, activities, and prayers. The first year focused on the family as the domestic church. They introduced, presented, and unpacked these themes: family Rosary; preparing for Advent; grace and holiness in family life; Epiphany and the Baptism of the Lord; preparing for Lent—making a plan, preparing for Holy Week; Easter—living the season fully; and, finally, Ascension and Pentecost. Each lesson included catechist guides, a training video, and a family guide. Lessons were available in English and Spanish and could be used in their entirety or as a supplemental tool in conjunction with the parish's chosen curriculum.

Faith conversations included questions to help guide seasonal practices:

- *For parents*: When you were growing up, how did your family prepare for Christmas during Advent?
- *For the whole family*: Which of the practices or traditions that you have experienced have brought you closer to God?

Faith conversations also included general questions that asked parents and children to reflect on issues of life and faith:

- Has your family experienced any of the ways that the time of COVID-19 has been like a desert? If yes, what are they?
- What are some good things that have happened during this time?
- What good have you gained from going through this experience together as a family, as a faith community?
- Do you think your family has grown closer to one another and/or to God?
- Is there anything holding you back from following Jesus with all your heart?

Faith practices included things like creating a sacred prayer space, family Rosary time, creating an Advent plan, or creating a spiritual plan for Lent.

The seasonal plans came with family guides. They offered instructional content and ideas on what that practice might look like when it is lived out. For example, the instructions for creating an Advent plan were outlined this way:

> After learning about the Spiritual and Corporal Works of Mercy, together decide which Works of Mercy your family will do this Advent. Don't feel you have to do all of them, because that's not practical. Some you may already do, like praying for the living and the dead. That's great! Keep doing those works and pick one or two more that fit naturally into your family life to do for Advent. Remember that Works of Mercy first begin at home within your family. Works of Mercy give us opportunities to love one another with God's love, and then to share that love by serving our neighbors. Next, make a Family Advent Plan that corresponds to what you have learned about the Works of Mercy. (www.evangelizationatl.com)

During the Easter season, families were instructed to choose an activity from the "Living Easter Season" suggestions. There were numerous suggestions for simple activities, such as these:

- Look at old photographs of departed loved ones and give thanks.
- It's okay to have questions. Read about "Doubting Thomas" (John 20:24–29).
- Take a fifteen-minute walk; carefully notice the things you see.

I love that they focused so intentionally on engaging every family in their diocese. I also love that their program defined four keys for practicing faith: 1) caring conversations, 2) family devotions and prayer, 3) family rituals and traditions, and 4) family service. They continue to develop this effort toward their ultimate goal: "to encourage families to pray together and grow together as disciples." Imagine if every family in your parish or your diocese was having faith conversations and was engaged in faith practices at home! These diocesan leaders provided their parish leaders with the flexibility and the adaptability they needed.

In the Office of Catechesis of the Archdiocese of Newark, this approach was called *Faith Alive @ Home: A Guide to Family Faith Worship and Family Faith Fun*. A section of this resource, Family Worship @ Home: Resources and Tips for Families, focused on how we might worship at home, celebrate the season at home, and pray with the Bible. For example, one Faith Alive @ Home issue provided ways to decrease distractions while watching mass at home. It also gave suggestions for how a family would create a home altar space and how they might use that sacred prayer space on a daily basis.

Another section, called Family Faith @ Home, offered ideas on how a parent might more confidently become the primary teacher of the faith at home. It expressed the importance of parents:

> As a parent, your role in the faith formation of your children is vital. No one can replace you, not even the best parish programs. Your parish community and the programs they offer exist to reinforce how you live faith at home. Recent studies show that if you are actively engaged with the practice of your faith, you greatly increase the probability that your children will be, too.

ENGAGE EVERY FAMILY

They formed families in the understanding that the family is the first school of discipleship, and in this they shared Pope Francis' repeated message to parents: "The family is the place where parents become the first teachers in the faith."

They affirmed fathers in a special summer issue for Father's Day. They honored St. Joseph and shared lessons we might glimpse from his example. They shared resources that expressed how dads give heroic witness to their children, suggested how moms can support dads in their role, and even pointed to the example of five saints who were great dads. All of this was focused on how we live the faith in our families, in our homes, in our daily lives—through faith conversations and faith practices.

Most of all, they gave parents support and encouragement to have faith conversations and to maintain or even start new faith practices. Some of the parent advice was geared toward faith topics; some was specific to parenting at home during quarantine, like this one from the Focus on the Faith website:

> These are unprecedented times — schedules are suddenly wide open and home, school, and work are jumbled up like never before. What an opportunity to learn, play, and grow with your children! They're watching you and need you now more than ever. This topsy-turvy time can be a gift. Make the most of it by connecting with your kids in new, meaningful ways. ("Parenting During the Coronavirus Crisis")

The leaders in this archdiocese also brought faith to real-life issues for parents. In the summer of 2020, when our country was experiencing incredible unrest amid protests against racism and racial injustice, they released a special Faith Alive @ Home issue focused on Catholic Social Teaching. Parents could explore each of the themes of Catholic Social Teaching with their children through the resources provided. In this issue, they were encouraged to talk with their children about racism, racial bias, diversity, and how and why we turn to God in times of challenge, loss, or tragedy. This issue also provided parents with prayer ideas, suggestions for action, and the example of saints who worked for justice. Materials came from across our Church: from publishers, the USCCB, Catholic Charities, and other organizations working for peace.

I share this because one of the graces that came from this time of focusing on the domestic church was that we didn't just provide facts about the faith. We weren't teaching children a prayer, but how to pray. Engaging parents meant we needed to make the faith relevant in what was happening in their lives at that exact moment. This is always true, but our response recognized this in ways it might not have done prior to the pandemic.

Finally, this archdiocese also created a special issue for families about the Synod on Synodality (2021–2023). Parents were presented with the idea of family synodality: creating a listening environment. The leaders curated articles like these: "Six Ways to Be a Better Listener at Home" and "Listening for Understanding: A Win-Win for Families." Then this issue unpacked what synodality means, what the synod is about, and how the family could participate in this listening process. So, not only did it focus on good practices and conversations at home, but it also affirmed that every family matters in the Church. What a great way to build bridges!

These are just two examples of how dioceses reached out to parents and families. Many other archdiocesan and diocesan leaders created similar resources to equip their own catechetical leaders for this work during this crisis. Some also offered resources directly to families.

- The Archdiocese of Detroit created *52 Sundays*, which it describes as "a dynamic guide to help you and your family reclaim the Lord's Day with prayer, activities, food, and more!"
- The Archdiocese of Seattle developed *At Home with Faith*, a resource that provides the Sunday readings, reflections, and conversation starters for families.

- The Diocese of Rochester shared a weekly digital newsletter, *The Family Zone*, focused on the lessons/themes of the upcoming Sunday readings. The newsletter included links to videos for young children and older children to watch with their family, discussion starters around the themes, reflections on the readings, and activities for the whole family. They also continued to curate on their Pinterest page in an effort to equip parents and help their professional leaders thrive in ministry.
- The Diocese of Trenton's *Faith at Home: Making Faith Come Alive for Your Families* focused on simple ideas. It offered ideas, tips, resources, and encouragement through the monthly column and podcast in the hope that families would continue to grow in the practice of the faith even when they weren't meeting regularly with their faith formation leaders.

I cannot provide an exhaustive list here; these are but a few examples. The way archdiocesan and diocesan offices stepped up to support the ministers in the field was extraordinary. Even more extraordinary were the individual stories of how families experienced all of this in their own parishes. This is where transformation was visible.

PARISH RESPONSES AND PROJECTS

As parish leaders recognized the need to equip parents, to make it easy, they quite naturally focused on faith conversations and faith practices. Some did this in the simplest of ways; others pivoted their entire programs. I spoke with leaders who put their programs on hold in the spring of 2020 and were not sure they had the resources to reach people in 2020 or 2021 in any real systemic, structural manner. Instead, they did what they could. They offered Advent kits, Lent kits—simple pick-up packets to help their families explore the faith during the Church season.

My husband and I witnessed the impact of just such efforts in our own parish. We volunteered, along with many other parishioners, to pack and distribute over a thousand Lent kits. We met in a parish hall, with masks and attending to good social distancing. In each kit, families received ashes, a candle, prayers, a music playlist, and more. As we delivered the kits, we met families on their porch steps, in their front yards, or in the entryway, all masked. We saw images on our parish's social media pages of parents putting ashes on their children's foreheads, lighting candles, and participating in the parish reconciliation service online. We were united. We were experiencing the Lenten season in a very special way. Children were connecting with parents around faith practices and through faith conversations. My own adult daughter, who lived with us for part of 2020 and 2021, posted images of her father giving us a blessing on Palm Sunday.

I talked to many leaders around the country who sent kits home. Volunteers and staff delivered kits to parishioners across their community. Some parishes held "car parades" or pick-up lines in their parking lots. These were very simple things, but they had the effect of bringing us all together in faith at a time when we could not physically be together for the liturgical celebrations of the season. One parent at a parish shared what it meant to be able to pick up palms on Palm Sunday:

> The kids and I decided it was very important for us to go to church and pick up the palms, since we were missing mass (in person) on Palm Sunday and Easter. My parents' faith is everything to them, and since they are in a compromised group for coronavirus, we decided that we would pick up palms for them as well and surprise them with the special delivery. In addition, we picked up one for my brother's family, whose church was not issuing palms, and dropped them off in the kids' Easter baskets on the porch. We did the same thing for our neighbor who was not able to get out. This was really special to us to be able to share the surprise with those that it means so much to.

Katie Neu, at that time the Director of Lifelong Faith Formation at the Catholic Community of St. Jude in New Lenox, Illinois, considered how their multi-component program could be reimagined to meet the needs of parents and families who couldn't gather in their family-centered faith formation program. Most of the program's components, besides the home lesson piece, were very much focused on gathering. Their *Explore 4* elective (focused on exploring the four pillars of faith outlined in the *Catechism of the Catholic Church*: creed, worship, Christian living, and Christian prayer) was a "life of the parish" component. Families chose to participate in four parish events each year, from a wide variety of ministries, events, and activities. We'll explore this elective-type curriculum more in Part Two of this book, but for this conversation, what the leaders of this parish needed to do was reimagine a component that was entirely dependent on gathered church activity. With the parish closed, ministries on hold, and events canceled, how could families reflect on what was happening in the "life of the parish"?

This faith formation team imagined *Explore 4 at Home*. They gave suggestions for what exploring the faith at home might look like, and they allowed families to come up with their own ideas as well. Katie said, "Already having parents teaching at home made transitioning to total faith formation at home so much easier for the staff and for the parents. I received *many emails* from parents saying how grateful they were for the resources we sent them and how appreciative they were of all the hard work we did." Families were grateful for efforts of the faith formation staff throughout the pandemic. They said they felt connected, cared for, and supported.

Families used the same reflection form for the *Explore 4 at Home* component as they had for the *Explore 4* gathered component. Families shared names, the activity, and the date of the activity, and then they answered the following questions:

- Describe the spiritual practice or activity you chose. Summarize what you did. Why did it interest you?
- How did this spiritual practice or activity help your family grow in your faith? Would you or why would you recommend it to others?

Katie said, "Too often we're afraid of expecting too much from parents, and if we just gave them books to teach their children and said, 'Here, finish the last three units and turn it in after you've completed the unit tests,' they might feel overwhelmed and possibly ill-equipped." But during the pandemic, she said, "if we can give parents the opportunities to pray with their children at home, to form their children in the faith by responding to their needs and their lives, real transformation is possible. Trust your parents. Trust the Holy Spirit!"

St. Jude staff trusted the parents and the Holy Spirit. These are just a few of the *Explore 4 at Home* reflections they received in 2020–2021:

> We chose to take a silent bike ride to the end of Blandford Avenue. From the end of the road, you can see a clear, open view of Silver Cross Hospital. We stopped, got off our bikes, and prayed for the patients suffering from COVID-19 that are in that hospital. We also prayed for the staff that is taking care of them. We ended with an Our Father. It was very emotional, considering what our world is experiencing right now. It helped us to have faith that God will get us through this very difficult time.

> We have been praying the Rosary as a family regularly during the quarantine. With extra time, it is no longer a challenge to "fit it in," and it has become part of our daily routine (on most days!). There is a version we like to pray together on EWTN. It is Fr. Pacwa's Holy Rosary in the Holy Land. Our girls enjoy it because there is a lot to see. They ask a lot of questions. For the most part, they cooperate! Praying the Rosary together is a beautiful family activity. I understand that the girls are not able to sustain perfect attention, but they are present and usually pray vocally. I feel that encouraging them to pray the Rosary sets a very good example, and they will remember doing it when they are older. Praying the Rosary has helped our girls learn a lot of prayers as well as the Mysteries of the Rosary. They are learning about the major events in the lives of Jesus and Mary and hopefully growing in their love of him.

As a family, we followed a scavenger hunt to find items from nature that would make the scene for the resurrection of Christ. The children had a fun time finding items outside and then working together to learn the importance of Jesus. It interested my family because we were able to do something as a family while learning about God in a fun way. It helped us to grow because after we put the objects together and read the Bible passage, everyone had a better perception of what the resurrection of Jesus meant. I would recommend this to others because it is a fun activity that involves teamwork to share God's word.

We did a prayer jar because every morning we wake up to such sad news. We say prayers for all the people that need it and prayers for all the good things that we still have going on in our lives and in the world. This is an ongoing activity....It's nice to hear the prayers of the kids and to hear what they are concerned about and how they are looking for God's help and guidance.

We started a gratitude box that is located in our living room. Sometimes I will prompt the kids to write things they are grateful for, especially if they are upset or complaining about something. Everyone in the family contributes throughout the week. Sunday night at dinner before we pray, we read the cards in the box. The kids like to guess who wrote which card. This is an ongoing activity; it is nice to hear the prayers of the kids and to hear what they are concerned about and how they are looking for God's help and guidance.

Today we decided to write messages of hope around our neighborhood. We have been doing it with chalk on our own driveway and today we wanted to take it out around three blocks so others can see. Writing expressions to give people a smile or just help them cope with everything going on today. It helps us grow because we spoke about people going through hard times or perhaps being lonely and what little things we can do to hope to cheer them up. Could even be as simple as a smile or an expression written. It was a great talking point for our family who are all younger, so it was nice way to speak about what is going on since two of the four of them don't really quite understand.

We have been listening to the kids' Catholic Sprouts Podcast every day together as a family and talking about it. It brings up a lot of questions among the kids. It also is a good connection to experiences in our own lives, such as death. We have lost two loved ones this year, and my kids have had a lot of questions.

We watched a short movie about the life of St. Augustine on Formed. I've been wanting to teach the kids more about the saints, and these videos are short and seem to keep their attention while providing some good lessons as well as Church history. After the video was over, we discussed the meaning of saints, what role they play in the Church, and how a saint becomes canonized. We also talked about how our Augustinian priests at St. Jude were derived from St. Augustine, and their focus, like his, was on teaching. Finally, we talked about his famous quote "Our hearts are restless until they rest in you." It's a good lesson for the kids that you can seemingly have everything—riches, power, etc.—but you cannot be truly happy until you let Jesus into your heart.

We all learned to pray the Rosary together as a family. It helped because of the coronavirus and how helpless it made us feel.... When you are restricted by social distancing, we decided that praying together was at least one way we could help.

Why do I share these stories? First, this is a piece we often miss and something that holds potential treasures—the reflections, the stories, the experience. We can give families activities to do, tasks to check off to be sure some requirement is met, but how can we let them know it matters to us? How can we let them know it's not just a hoop to jump through? This parish got it right when they asked families to share their stories and then turned around and shared some of those stories with the wider parish community—anonymously, unless permission to share names was given. Since this parish implemented this component years ago, they have often shared these reflections, and sometimes images, in their faith formation newsletters and on their social media pages. They also shared the reflections in bulletins and on their website. They shared these stories in parent gatherings, during parent panel discussions, building a kind of "positive peer pressure."

Second, I share these stories because this practice uplifts the catechetical leader. You don't have to wonder if a family is participating in faith conversations and practices: you are a witness to that participation, to their stories, to moments of growth and transformation. This is one of the questions I get most often. How do you know families are doing these activities? How do you hold them accountable? Telling them it's mandatory and having them check off a list of requirements might not make a difference, but creating a culture of storytelling, of reflecting and sharing those experiences, will.

And finally, these reflections offer a glimpse into what is possible when families are given ownership over at least part of their faith formation plan. We'll look at that further in lesson 5, on encouraging families to create their own faith formation plans.

Questions for Reflection

1. Two things have the greatest impact on the faith formation of young people: God-talk and faith conversations. This is where archdiocesan, diocesan, and parish leaders excelled during the pandemic. How did your ministry focus on encouraging and equipping faith conversations and faith practices in families?

2. How might this experience lead us to form our faith communities in the need to engage families in faith formation? How might we build that support for this effort?

3. What stories did you hear from families about how they practiced the faith or grew in faith during this time?

4. What methods did you implement for families to share their experiences? If this was not a part of your ministry efforts during this time, how might it be in the future?

5. If you curated reflections/stories from families, how did you share those stories with the parish community? If you did not, how might you do so in the future?

6. How do you build trust (among leaders and catechists) in parents' capacity to embrace their role as primary teachers or primary witnesses of the faith?

7. How do you support parents in this effort?

8. How might you help families unpack the experience of Church and/or faith formation they have had during this crisis? How could that exercise be formational?

9. What resonates in this exploration of lesson 3? What challenges you? Or what would you challenge?

LESSON 4
CONNECT PARENTS TO OTHERS

> Connect parents to one another
> and to the larger faith community.

During the COVID shutdown, congregations offered a wide variety of small groups for parents, including affinity groups arranged by children's ages, by children's or teens' needs, or by topics. Parents were comforted and encouraged as they realized they were not alone in their experience of teaching their children at home while working from home or navigating childcare and COVID-19 safety precautions. This also led to discussions about moments of grace, or gratitude, or naming where they saw God working in their lives. We've only begun to explore the many ways this is possible and the many benefits to providing such connection.

We've all heard someone complain (or maybe we were the one complaining) about the parents who are willing to spend all day on a Saturday at the soccer field, or a whole weekend at a volleyball tournament, or a Friday night at a dance recital, but are resistant to join

In virtue of their baptism, all the members of the People of God have become missionary disciples (cf. Matthew 28:19). All the baptized, whatever their position in the Church or their level of instruction in the faith, are agents of evangelization, and it would be insufficient to envisage a plan of evangelization to be carried out by professionals while the rest of the faithful would simply be passive recipients. The new evangelization calls for personal involvement on the part of each of the baptized.

■ *Pope Francis,* **Evangelii Gaudium, #120**

a parent gathering or even come to a parent meeting. We may have been frustrated at some point with the parent who will allow their child to skip a catechetical session due to a sporting event. But we need to stop pointing fingers and start asking questions that might help us address that issue. Why are parents willing to spend all those hours at the field, or at the court, or at a dance recital? Sure, parents want to support their children, but another reason is that parents have built relationships with the other parents. Together they talk about their children—their dreams, their fears, and their hopes for their kids. They talk about the struggles in raising their children. They share the celebrations. They've made strong relationships, some lifelong, on those fields and in those studios. Where have we offered that kind of hospitality? Where might we be able to create space for parents to develop relationships with other parents? I've seen it done in parishes in powerful ways. That is transformative ministry: transformative for the family, the community, even for you, the ministry leader.

Kathie Amidei is an author, a presenter, and a pastoral associate on the Parish Leadership Team at St. Anthony on the Lake in Pewaukee, Wisconsin. I've spoken with Kathie and her pastor, Fr. Tony Zimmer, about their family program numerous times through the years. Over ten years ago, I visited St. Anthony looking for inspiration and the wisdom of a leader who had successfully made this paradigm shift to a family-centered approach to faith formation. I was both affirmed in what we had started and challenged to do more. St. Anthony had been offering a family approach focused on lifelong faith formation for almost twenty years by then (now over twenty-five years). I participated in a session that first visit, sitting with families with young children. I asked families about their experiences. Every response was positive. This was a part of their culture and already a long-standing tradition.

When the pandemic left many parishes trying to figure out how to deliver content digitally, Kathie's team was trying to figure out how to gather families safely. Before long, the team added an extra session each month to accommodate the need for more space. Families met in small groups in every space available throughout their campus, at safe physical distances and masked. Parents expressed gratitude to the parish staff for the opportunity to be with one another, to not be isolated during such difficult times. In addition to meeting once a month in person, the same group of families met virtually with a facilitator from the parish for a Family Program session from their homes, with materials at hand. There were gifts in this process that Kathie and her team said they might not have discovered if there hadn't been a need for this creativity. These pods of families gave parents an opportunity to get to know one another, to share their experiences. They celebrated the resilience of their community of faith.

This lifelong faith approach is such a part of their culture at St. Anthony that at the request of veterans of the program (parents who had been through it with their children), they offer an "Emeritus" opportunity for adults who wish to continue in the program to gather for fellowship, formation, and faith sharing. They meet at the same time as the family program. The website describes it as a cohort of adults who are interested in the further development of their faith: "Our time together will include catechesis, prayer, and time for discussion—so we can learn from each other and create community. It's like Family Program without the pipe cleaners and glitter glue!"

CREATE SPACE

In my early years as a director of a family faith formation program, it took us a while to discover the benefits of allowing parents time to talk with each other. We wanted to make sure parents knew the doctrinal material enough to teach their children and to support what we taught. If you had visited us in those early days, you would have seen an example of what *not* to do. Parents and children gathered. We opened with prayer and a few words about the theme of the month, then the children were dismissed with their catechists to their classrooms. We proceeded to "teach" (you should hear "lecture" here) the parents for the next hour. Until we discovered a better way.

We implemented a pattern of changing up speakers, starting in prayer (a modified *lectio divina*), followed by a shorter presentation mixed with video, conversations, and some speaking. We added lots of hospitality and opportunities for parents to speak to one another. We were amazed at what they learned from each other, which was probably more than they learned from us. As I presented one afternoon in 2013, we spoke about our new pope, Pope Francis, and his emphasis on mercy. We showed clips of John Allen Jr. speaking about this. I spoke of the sacrament of reconciliation: "I don't know how you feel about the sacrament of reconciliation," I said. "I consider it a gift, such incredible mercy, but I haven't always." As I shared my previous resistance, I told them of an experience of reconciliation I had when my husband and I were youth ministers. We were at a youth conference. There were probably thirty priests lined up around the field house of the university to hear the confessions of hundreds of teens. We had a few young people who were not lining up, so my husband nudged me and said, "Get in line." I gave him a look, told *him* to get in line, and then begrudgingly moved in the direction he pointed. I liked participating in the sacrament when I had prepared, when it was quiet and tucked away, not out in the middle of a field house with hundreds of noisy teens.

There were two priests closest to us: one jolly, laughing young priest, and another stern-looking, very serious older priest. I told the parents at this family session that of course I got in line with the younger, laughing priest and tried to avoid eye contact with the other. The parents laughed as I described the line with the older priest moving faster and me trying to avoid eye contact, looking everywhere but his direction, until...not one person was left in his line, and there were still five young people ahead of me. I sat down in the chair opposite this serious priest I had never seen before and have never seen since. I went through my "laundry list" of sins: being angry with my husband, impatient with my children, judgmental of my neighbor....The priest cut me off, saying, "My dear, what's on your heart?"

I had never shared this experience with others. It happened years ago, in 2004, at the height of the abuse scandal in our diocese. I told the priest that I was angry with Church leadership, with our bishop even, for the pain caused, the mistakes made, the words chosen when speaking to the local media, and, if I was honest, for making my job as a minister more difficult. I told the priest that some days, I was having difficulty even praying. I continued to unburden my heart. I don't remember the words he said, but I'll never forget his gaze, his kindness and mercy, and how it washed over me. He was truly Jesus for me in that moment. I hadn't realized how angry I was until he asked so sincerely, "What's on your heart?"

When I shared this experience with parents, I was surprised, even embarrassed, at the emotion in my voice and the tears that streamed down my cheeks. How could they spill like this nine years later? I had never been so vulnerable in front of our parents.

I quickly moved them into small groups, as I apologized for the emotion and tried to move on. I don't remember the discussion questions on the table, but I do remember that whatever they were, parents were talking about times they struggled with faith, with sacraments, or moments when they found it difficult to pray. I walked around, collecting myself as I listened to their conversations. I heard the concern in their voices and saw parents crying. One dad shared his own anger about the abuse scandal, then expressed gratitude for having a safe place to name his doubts, concerns, and struggles. Prior to this, he had spoken only to friends and neighbors who simply asked him why he stayed and even encouraged him to leave the Church, as they had. One divorced mom cried as she shared how hard it was some days to stay in the Church, feeling judged for the failure of her marriage and worried whether her children would share her faith. She was grateful to share her story and have others offer compassion and understanding. Sharing had not changed her situation, but it allowed her to navigate it for the moment—because she felt less alone. Another woman shared that she, too, was hurting. Every time she walked into a church, she felt like she was betraying her gay sister. If she stayed away from church, she felt like she was betraying God. She vacillated between the two. She knew she disappointed other family members who had since turned away from the Church in support of their sister. Parents hugged one another; some exchanged contact information. Something changed that day. In them and in me.

It is amazing what happens when we just create space and trust the Holy Spirit. Many programs follow the children's curriculum, like the two programs described above, offering conversation around the topics the young people are learning about. But some parishes have taken a different approach, offering parent affinity groups for parents of teens, or parents of young children, or parents of children with special needs, or parents of children who identify as LGBTQ. These parishes meet parents where they are, then offer some faith sharing and learning, but also with parenting support.

Recently, I visited the Archdiocese of New York and met a father from a parish in New York City. This faith community has offered a family approach to faith formation for well over a decade, but instead of parents focusing on the children's curriculum and the staff driving the conversation in the parent groups, they allow the parents to facilitate the group. They offer the same prompt each week: "How are you doing...really?" The father who described this said you don't need to overplan, you don't need to script anything, you simply need to give parents space. All of the big stuff comes up—and it's not all pain, he said. There are great moments of celebration and joy. They share world stuff, Church stuff, family stuff, all wrapped in faith. He shared that he had never felt more like he belonged than when he began participating in family faith formation. Growing up in a small Midwest Catholic parish, he never felt like he belonged. He was looking for community when he came to this New York City parish and found it. He described what happened in this monthly parent gathering as "restoration." Parents were not just being served (treated the same as the kids, receiving services and leaving when it was done); they were serving one another. They were being called to leadership roles. This had connected them to other parents and to the community at large.

ACCOMPANIMENT

People need to talk about their hopes, dreams, pain, and suffering. They need fellow travelers who share the journey of faith (and parenting). Where do we offer this type of accompaniment in our parishes and programs? We are called to this ministry of building bridges of trust so that, hopefully, the brokenness in our Church doesn't keep them from growing in greater intimacy with Christ.

In his book *Sacred Companions: The Gift of Spiritual Friendship and Direction*, David G. Benner makes a bold statement: "If you are making significant progress on the transformational journey of Christian spirituality, you have one or more friendships that support that journey. If you do not, you are not. It is that simple." There's a reason we're called to community. We need one another. "Ours is a deeply personal faith," says Benner, "but it was never meant to be private."

He goes on to tell the story of a friend who was not happy with his church but continued to go. When Benner asked why, he said, "Church keeps me in touch with others on the spiritual journey. Spiritual growth is just too hard to maintain alone." We need one another. We need the witness of those who have gone before us. We need the companionship of those who walk with us today. Benner says, "Intimate relationships with others prepare us for intimacy with God." Do you have a friend who will ask the question "How are you doing? No, really, how are you doing?" and dare to go deeper for the answer? What would happen if we created that kind of safe and sacred space in our communities?

Having a spiritual companion on the journey has helped me through those challenging times, calling me back to my greatest call: to remember I am loved by God. "The task of spiritual friends is to help us discern the presence, will, and leading of the Spirit of God." If we create the kind of space that allows this relationship building in our programs, our families and our communities will be reminded of their greatest call: to remember they are loved by God. And that makes all the difference.

Questions for Reflection

1. In what ways have you offered hospitality to parents?

2. Have you created space for parents to connect to other parents? If so, how have you done that? If not, how might you offer this space in the future?

3. If you haven't created this space for connection, do you experience any resistance to this parent-focused ministry? If yes, how might you work through that?

4. After creating the space for parents to connect, how do you encourage them to build relationships with one another and with the broader community?

5. As you plan for a parent ministry, will it be done according to the curriculum of the children? Will it be focused on grouping parents according to children's ages or needs? Or will it be more loosely defined, allowing parents to facilitate that space themselves? How will you discern which approach you take? Will you include parents in this discernment?

6. Author David Benner says, "If you are making significant progress on the transformational journey of Christian spirituality, you have one or more friendships that support that journey. If you do not, you are not. It is that simple." Do you agree or disagree?

7. What resonates in this exploration of lesson 4? What challenges you? Or what would you challenge?

LESSON 5
ENCOURAGE FAMILIES TO CREATE PLANS AND SHARE EXPERIENCES

> Encourage families to create their own faith formation plan (or a portion of it), then invite them to share their experiences.

Many ministry leaders equipped families with curated "playlists" as a kind of idea bucket from which families could create their own plans for spurring faith conversations and practices at home. A family could choose activities and lessons according to their children's ages, spiritual interests, or even family schedules. This strategy leads us away from a one-size-fits-all approach and encourages us to meet each person or family where they are.

Yet the first and most important place for passing on the faith is the home. It is in the home that we learn to believe, through the quiet daily example of parents who love our Lord and trust in his word. There, in the home, which we can call the "domestic church", children learn the meaning of fidelity, integrity and sacrifice. They see how their mother and father interact with each other, how they care for each other and for others, how they love God and love the Church. In this way, children can breathe in the fresh air of the Gospel and learn to understand, judge and act in a manner worthy of the legacy of faith they have received. The faith, brothers and sisters, is passed on "around the family table", at home in ordinary conversation, in the language that persevering love alone knows how to speak.

■ *Pope Francis, World Meeting of Families, Ireland, August 25–26, 2018*

VIRTUAL FAMILY OF BELIEVERS:
MAIN COURSE AND SIDE DISHES

One example of this kind of effort is the joint project Virtual Family of Believers. This was a collaboration between the parish leaders at Ss. John and Paul Parish in Altoona, Iowa; the directors at the Diocese of Des Moines; and St. Joseph Educational Center, with its director, my friend and colleague Tom Quinlan. Tom was the Director of the Diocese of Joliet when I was in parish ministry and my supervisor when I worked with the diocese. He has long advocated for family catechesis. In this collaborative effort, described as a "family or inter-generational approach to parish faith formation, digitally delivered, during a pandemic," parents were equipped to lead their family's faith formation at home.

Ss. John and Paul Parish had offered an intergenerational faith formation program for seventeen years prior to the pandemic. They quickly realized they would have to adapt their program to deliver faith formation virtually. Each month, households gathered virtually for a forty-minute session. These Zoom sessions were offered twice each month and recorded for those who could not attend. Households then visited the Virtual Family of Believers website to choose from a menu of activities that supported the lesson each month. All households were asked to engage with a few of the components (the "main course"). They customized the rest of their monthly plan by choosing from a variety of "side dishes" and "desserts." That variety was offered so that families could choose activities according to the ages, interests, and abilities of their members.

I asked the parish leaders at Ss. John and Paul to share with me what they learned. Jenni Lihs, Coordinator of Faith Formation for the parish, said, "We learned that we had to continue to interact and stay involved with households. We probably did this better online then we have done at any other time. Each session was an intentional dis-cussion about what the parish connection was for each month, how to incorporate it, and how we could include feedback and interaction from during the L!VE session." I was impressed with the intentionality they practiced in connecting the church of the home and the church of the community—domestic church and parish.

Jenni went on to say, "One thing we learned from Virtual Family of Believers and gathering on Zoom was to invite and include households in the different aspects of the session. Whether that was recording the prayer sequence, the gathering sequence, trying break-out sessions, doing Kahoots (online response polls), or having the families complete a project and then send a picture [of that]...we made a video of [it] and then shared [that]. It was important to include different households in different manners and to stay connected."

Paulette Chapman added, "We were able to reach households that had not been very engaged previously. A virtual option offers some possibilities for the future for other reasons as well. It provides an alternative for households with members with special needs when they're not up to attending in person, and it gives a 'make-up' option when illness strikes. Our catechists are with children and youth while their parents and other adults have a guest speaker; recording and posting that session gives those catechists access to the adult gathering later. One size does not fit all and the need to be creative taught us there are many ways to customize faith formation."

SEASONAL FAITH FORMATION PLANS
Another example of that approach is St. Benedict Catholic Church in the Galveston-Houston Diocese. Their stated goal for Whole Family Catechesis is to support the family and their faith formation journey. Matthew Crews, Director of Evangelization at St. Benedict, has led this paradigm shift. He said the pandemic accelerated their five-year plan, but he believes that was a gift. He also acknowledged that it was important to keep in mind the families' different experiences and to let families have some ownership over their faith formation plans. One way the parish did that in 2022 was to help families create their own Lenten plan. Families gathered at the parish around tables. The leaders provided materials, including family activities (focused on prayer, sacrifice, and almsgiving), Lenten prayers, recipes for meatless meals, and

videos about Lent. Families outlined what they would do individually and together to grow spiritually throughout Lent. Matthew talked with one family, a mother and daughter, about Lenten fasting as they shared that they have been vegetarian for a couple of years. "It hardly seems like fasting to give up meat on Fridays," the mom said. A conversation about sacrifice and the intention of fasting ensued. By the time they were done talking, the mom and daughter had determined what would be a meaningful fast for both of them. This year, Lent would be a growing experience for them and for each of the families who created their own spiritual growth plans for Lent.

ANNUAL THEMES

In 2020–2021, St. Catherine of Siena Catholic Church focused on the annual theme "Living Leisurely through the Liturgical Year." What a great theme for a year when families were experiencing leisure and Sabbath in new ways in the midst of the pandemic. An introduction video/podcast on "The Art of Leisure" explored what leisure is and what it is not. It is not just what we do when we're not working. Leisure is necessary for peace and for prayer. Families explored the theme by completing homework from the age-appropriate workbooks and then choosing a family project from a number of activities. Those activities might include a family-friendly movie on the subscription site Formed, or an activity from their St. Catherine's liturgical cooking series, "Faith, Family and Food!"—available on YouTube. This series was focused on cooking together and enjoying a family meal while celebrating a liturgical feast day. They kicked off the year with the feast of St. Hildegard of Bingen, on September 17. Families learned that St. Hildegard kept an extensive list of foods she liked and foods she didn't like. One item in the first meal was "meatballs braised in beer," which St. Hildegard reportedly really enjoyed. Movie night or a cooking contest: what a great way to engage families! We are called to evangelize with joy, to catechize with joy, and this is an example of what that might look like.

In 2021–2022, St. Catherine's continued to offer options for family projects even as they gathered monthly. The children used Pflaum's

Gospel Weeklies for age-appropriate lessons, and the parish offers many choices now for the family projects. For example, in January, families could choose between a video from Formed (different options for families with younger children or older youth), a podcast, an Epiphany blessing of the home, "Faith, Family, and Food!" "Carrying Hope" (a backpack for a child in crisis), or prayer (honoring Mary in the home prayer space). Families shared their responses to the questions about the experiences or sent in photographs of their family meals, prayer space, and so on. Sharing those stories builds community. Families are able to see what other families were doing. This helps them get to know one another and to become the storytellers of their own faith life. It also promotes positive peer pressure. Allowing families to choose their plan gives ownership over their own spiritual and faith formation growth. What a great way to acknowledge that one size does not fit all.

A "LIFE OF THE PARISH" COMPONENT

The Catholic Community of St. Jude has encouraged families to create their own faith formation plan (at least in part) for over ten years now. They began offering a multi-component program in 2009. The elective component was one piece of the puzzle. The family program consisted of three primary parts: 1) a gathered component, 2) a family or home component, and 3) a community or "life of the parish" component. This third component was birthed after an intensive study of the U.S. bishops' 1999 pastoral plan, *Our Hearts Were Burning Within Us* (see chapter 5 for a description of that study). The parish leadership created this elective opportunity after reflecting on the bishops' statement that "The parish *is* the curriculum" (OHWB, #118). They created a parish network of formators by speaking to ministry leaders, asking what ministry offerings, events, or services the leaders wished families would participate in. They prepared those ministries to welcome families. They helped those ministries prepare families to participate. St. Jude called this elective component *Explore 4*, since it focused on exploring the four pillars of the faith as defined by the *Catechism of the Catholic Church* (creed, prayer, sacraments, and morality).

This allowed families to choose parish devotions, events, and ministries that spoke to their own spirituality. This component would put parents not only in contact with, but also in relationship with, other adults in the parish. Families would meet people who were on fire for the faith and passionate about the ministry they were engaged in, whether that was Rosary for Life on Wednesday evenings or Saturday mornings, or the annual Peace and Social Justice World Hunger event. Families chose four events each year (thus the name "Explore 4") to participate in and then to reflect on; afterward, they would share their responses to a few questions:

- Describe the spiritual practice or activity you chose. Summarize what you did.
- Why did it interest you?
- How might this spiritual practice or activity help your family grow in faith?
- List possible benefits of participating in this parish event as a member of the parish.

Again, this reflection increases that sense of ownership. When asked, "What counts?" the faith formation team determined that everything counts! They allowed for one social elective each year (the parish picnic, fish fry, etc.), but otherwise everything counted: prayer and devotions, service activities, learning opportunities, everything. This manner of connecting family to the parish helped build relationships and strengthen the community. Through the years, the leadership team shared the family reflections in the bulletin, in the newsletter, on the faith formation Facebook page, or at a parent event. This sharing affirms the families, treats them as the valuable contributing members of the faith community that they are, empowers them as the tellers of their own stories, and offers them space as evangelizers in their family and their parish.

Early on, a mom shared this reflection. She chose to take her three boys (around six, eight, and nine years old) to the Stations of the

Cross one Friday night during Lent. She said she chose the Stations of the Cross because she knew she could get in and out in thirty minutes or less. Nothing was required of her or her boys other than following along. She knew she wouldn't feel uncomfortable or out of place because she had prayed the Stations of the Cross at her childhood parish with her aunt many times growing up. It was a part of their family's Lenten ritual. As this mom participated in the Stations of the Cross with her boys, she began to feel emotional. She said it was like Catholic muscle memory...all these memories coming back, including the time spent with an aunt who had since died. Her boys wondered what was wrong, and she told them about her aunt and this practice. It was then that she realized her boys had never attended the Stations of the Cross. They didn't have what she had growing up. She said it was like a lightbulb going on. Now she understood why the Church calls on parents to form their children in faith, why families are called to *live* the faith, not just *learn about* the faith. Her sharing her story with the community helped other parents understand. It builds a sense of "we are in this together" and "I don't have to do this alone." They are the community. They are the Church. When parents have these moments of realization and share them, they become the biggest advocates for your program. It is reciprocal, and this "life of the parish" approach is focused on that reciprocal relationship that the *Directory for Catechesis* speaks of:

> The Church proclaims the Gospel to the family. The Christian community is a family of families and is itself the family of God. Community and family are, each for the other, a constant and reciprocal point of reference: while the community receives from the family an understanding of the faith that is immediate and connected in a natural way to the affairs of life, the family in turn receives from the community an explicit key for using faith to reinterpret its experience. Aware of this profound connection, the Church, in her devotion to evangelization, proclaims the Gospel to families, showing them by experience that

this is "joy that 'fills hearts and lives,' because in Christ we have been 'set free from sin, sorrow, inner emptiness and loneliness.'" (#229)

The community is enlivened by the family, and the family finds meaning in community.

Questions for Reflection

1. What is your response to allowing families to accept the responsibility of creating a faith formation plan?

2. If you employed this strategy, would you choose a seasonal approach or a component approach, like a "life of the parish" component?

3. Take a survey of the prayer opportunities and the learning, service, and social opportunities in your faith community. How might you create a network of parish formators with a "life of the parish" component? What would it look like in your parish?

4. Name one or more people in leadership roles in ministry whom you would want to collaborate with in this type of approach (someone whose faith is on fire, who is passionate about their ministry).

5. If you plan to employ a seasonal approach, what season or feasts will you focus on in the first year?

6. How will you curate the plans or the experiences of your families?

7. What resonates in this exploration of lesson 5? What challenges you? Or what would you challenge?

LESSON 6
BUILD OR STRENGTHEN COMMUNITY THROUGH STORYTELLING

> Build or strengthen community through storytelling.
> Be sure to include digital storytelling.

I loved bedtime when I was younger because it was synonymous with story time. My parents read to us every night. In her book *Listening to God's Word*, Alice Camille says, "Next to actually living, telling stories is probably our most important activity." People need stories. "'Tell me a story,'" says Camille, "is one of the first refrains of childhood, and despite our advancing years, we never stop asking for more....Our insatiable appetite for stories is a good thing. Stories tell us who we are and why we are."

Stories are the way we pass on our faith to the next generation. Humans have done this since the beginning of time. Stories are the way we come to know another person. They are how we make sense of experience. We live and breathe stories every day, all day. Stories are the deepest way that we can connect with another person. It's like Brené Brown says when she speaks of vulnerability: the two most powerful words when we are struggling are "Me too." Someone understands. We feel seen. In "Our Personal Stories Matter for Our Mental Health," social scientist Jonathan Adler says, "A large body of research suggests that there is a connection between the story of our lives—

The language that has the greatest hold on the digital generation is that of the story, rather than that of argumentation.
■ **Directory for Catechesis, #363**

our narrative identity—and our mental health."[4] Stories connect us to ourselves, to others, and to God. Stories impact our spirituality. A story is how we make sense of experiences, of transitions, even of life and death. When we create space for storytelling, we build empathy; we build community.

Woven throughout all of the lessons we've explored should be the idea that we need to equip our people as evangelizers. Let them share their experiences in their own words and images. During the COVID crisis, churches created community through social media posts, images, faith conversation starters, information, encouragement, and hashtags (like #ChurchName, #StillTogether), allowing members to participate and share their own images, ideas, and reflections.

I've shared my experience as a parishioner of Old St. Patrick's in Chicago. Throughout the crisis, I felt connected in powerful ways because of Instagram, hashtags, parish podcasts, and staff-driven communications around the liturgy and other virtual events at the parish. But my parish is not the only one that got creative in how it employed storytelling strategies, and specifically storytelling, to unite people and to build or strengthen their communities. These are two methods that are easy to repeat:

- Sharing stories on the parish website, in the bulletin, by email, and on social media pages like Facebook, Instagram, Twitter, and more
- Curating or creating podcasts or videos that tell the stories of the people in the community

One of the parishes I worked with through Vibrant Faith's calling initiative adapted the questions asked in the Rite of Christian Initiation of Adults to create a process around such storytelling:

---

4   https://spsp.org/news-center/blog/our-personal-stories-matter-our-mental-health

- What did you see?
- What did you feel?
- What did you learn?

As they planned to reopen, they made sure to include storytelling opportunities to allow their community to connect to one another, to the community as a whole, and to their faith in God. Storytelling provides an experience of processing the grief, the isolation, the loss, the lessons of the pandemic, and even the gifts they may have experienced during this great pause. Where was God at work in their lives? These were themes they could explore with those three simple questions.

Another parish that was engaged in this project infused storytelling into almost everything they did. They asked families to share images of the family faith projects they did at home, then shared those images on their Instagram and Facebook pages. They asked parishioners to share reflections during Advent for their "Word of the Day—Advent" practice. They shared parishioners' reflections for Lent the same way. One of the reflections starts off this way: "How can I find gladness in mourning? How can I find wholeness in sorrow? Working as an ER nurse in March 2020, I could not bring myself to ask these questions." Each reflection throughout Lent is a very personal, very vulnerable story. They are not anonymous stories. These parishioners are getting to know one another. Where once Advent and Lenten Vespers were led by the pastor, other priests, or staff, now people from the pews were invited to lead these liturgies.

This same parish had talked about story prior to the pandemic. As part of our calling initiative, they were brainstorming what a podcast might look like. We talked about StoryCorps, a nonprofit story-curating organization founded by Dave Isay. The mission of this organization is to "preserve and share humanity's stories in order to build connections between people and create a more just and compassionate world." Many of their stories are housed at the American Folklife Center at the Library of Congress in Washington, D.C. Isay wrote *Listening Is an Act of Love* about this mission. We also discussed the popularity of the social media-driven "Humans of New York," an effort that began as a photography project by author, photographer, and blogger Brandon Stanton.

The leadership at St. Charles Borromeo parish imagined an effort that told the stories of those in their community as a way of building community, understanding, empathy, and a sense of calling. The podcast was imagined before the pandemic and born a few months in. "From Where I Stand" was created on Anchor (a free digital tool that makes podcasts easy) and is introduced this way:

> Sometimes, in the most ordinary moment, we see life in a different way. It's the moment when you realize that you are being called to some new choice. Here, we'll share the story of someone who has experienced a call. Their life might be just like yours; or nothing like it. But as you listen, you might find yourself realizing, "I've been called too"...From Where I Stand.[5]

The stories were diverse, and yet there was this thread that ran through them all: "Where is God working in your life, or where is God calling you?" Joe shared his story about how he has been called during the times of COVID-19 to serve others as an EMT. Michele and Tatiana shared their experience as a mother and a daughter from a biracial family during the times of the civil unrest in our country. Lexi shared her call to work with those who are incarcerated. Dan and Jenny shared their call to be married during this time of pandemic. Dominique and Dave, a young newly married couple, shared what it is like to be expecting their first child during COVID. One family shared how they live a life of faith as a family, especially in an online world during the pandemic. Helen, her mother, Nonny, and her daughter, Grace, share about the call to motherhood and how the relationships of mother/daughter and grandmother/granddaughter have helped them to grow and to experience God's loving presence.

---

5 https://anchor.fm/st-charles-borromeo

This was powerful storytelling. It builds community. It helps parishioners know a little more about someone in their community and, in the process, often strengthens faith. Their pastor recently reflected:

> The novelist Eudora Welty once observed, "long before I wrote stories, I listened for stories." Listening for stories....To be a disciple of the Lord involves the willingness to serve, forgive, show compassion, work for justice, and embrace a spiritual life....
> I think it also involves the willingness to listen for stories.

They have created a culture of storytelling, which surely promotes a culture of lifelong faith formation.

The more I've focused on stories in recent years, the more I began to explore all the ways we tell stories in our parishes—how we share our faith, our lives, our hope: proclaiming God's word, homilies, witness talks, opportunities for parishioners to share reflections (in the bulletin, in the newsletter, in parent sessions, at Vespers, etc.), mentoring opportunities, teaching, in print (bulletins, emails, social media, etc.), and even how we tell stories with our buildings, our statues, and so on. As you consider this, think about where, in those stories, you hear celebrations of humanity, stories of hope, stories of repentance and renewal. Think of where you experience wonder and awe. Begin to imagine how you might use those opportunities to inspire, to build community, to offer healing and hope.

This lesson, this strategy, isn't one that requires you to change everything you're doing in your faith formation approach, in your program. It simply implies that you infuse the spirit of storytelling into what you're already doing—at every opportunity.

Questions for Reflection

1. Where and how do you hear stories in your community?

2. Where in those stories do you hear celebration of humanity, stories of hope, stories of repentance and renewal?

3. Where do you experience wonder and awe in your community?

4. How might you inspire hope and healing in your ministry?

5. How might you inspire faith practice? How might you inspire families to live the faith?

6. Spiritual writer and poet Mark Nepo says, "All things are connected. The art of community is discovering how." What does this mean? How do you practically apply this to a strategy of storytelling?

7. If you were to create a podcast, who (in your community) would you collaborate with? Who would you interview? How might you prepare parishioners to tell their stories? What questions might you ask?

8. In chapter 2, lesson 1, I shared my experience in my own parish, which used hashtags to build a sense of community on social media (#WeareOSP). Other communities did the same (#AnchoredInFaith, #stclementsschoolchicago, etc.). Have you employed this strategy? If yes, what response are you getting from your parish? How could you build on that? If not, how might you employ this strategy? What hashtags might you use to encourage participation in a social media campaign?

9. What resonates in this exploration of lesson 6? What challenges you? Or what would you challenge?

PART TWO

Guiding Essentials to Integrated Faith Formation

Faith grows when it is lived and shaped by love. That is why our families, our homes, are true domestic churches. They are the right place for faith to become life, and life to grow in faith.

POPE FRANCIS, WORLD MEETING OF FAMILIES, SEPTEMBER 27, 2015

The ministry of evangelization carried out by Christian parents is original and irreplaceable. It assumes the characteristics typical of family life itself, which should be interwoven with love, simplicity, practicality and daily witness.

ST. JOHN PAUL II, *FAMILIARIS CONSORTIO, #53*

THREE

Connecting with Parents: Reimagining Parent Meetings

We grew and expanded our understanding of what faith formation can be in the future in so many ways, but one of the greatest lessons we learned was to be in relationship with parents. We are called to accompany parents, to walk with them and empower them to be the spiritual leaders of their families. We need to encourage them by meeting them where they are, affirming what they're already doing well, and equipping them in ways that help them grow further. I have always had such a heart for parents, especially those who are struggling to live their faith, those who want to but aren't sure how, and those who are unchurched but desire this faith for their children. There are many parents now, some Generation X, some Millennials, who were baptized in the faith but never really learned or lived the faith. Still, they're showing up: they're registering their children for faith formation or for sacraments, and for that, we need to acknowledge their efforts. *They are being countercultural just by showing up!* I have found that when we walk with them, affirm them, and build up their confidence, amazing things happen. Most are already doing more than we give them credit for. Let's focus on that and build them up further. If we keep focusing on what they're not doing, or what they don't do well enough, they may not continue to make the effort.

Parents may or may not have ever encountered Christ in their journey, but if they are with us, our mission has to be to help them meet or get to know better the person of Jesus. If we keep blaming parents and setting up an "us and them" push and pull, we are not living up to our own calling. We have no more excuses. If we did not know before, even after all the research, the importance of parents, we certainly do after the experience of the last couple of years.

In the fall of 2021, I attended a parent orientation at a church that's been innovating in family faith formation for some time. As we greeted families, I welcomed parents back and asked moms and dads how they were doing. I listened to their stories. There were parents whose work required them to return to the office at least a few days a week, and they weren't sure how they were going to manage daycare. Others had children who needed rides to and from school because bus driver vacancies had yet to be filled. Still others decided to homeschool their children because of issues that arose over wearing masks or not. Some had moved their own parents into their households to care for them. They were carrying so much, and if I'm honest, they looked like it. I held them all in prayer as I looked around the worship space.

Around the same time, I read an article in *The Atlantic* that painted a stark picture. The title was "Parents Are Not Okay." The author, Dan Sinker, wrote: "We're not even at a breaking point anymore. We're broken." Parents are navigating so many variables; if we're expecting things to go back to "normal" anytime soon, we will be disappointed. We have to change the conversation. Again, I think of Jesus and his example of ministry. In his call to the disciples in the first chapter of the book of John, as they follow him, he turns and asks, "What are you looking for?"

Almost every parent before you is there for one reason: their children. They want their children to "have what they had." In working with parents, I've heard that again and again, and after some time in family-focused ministries, parents realize that their children do not have what they had. Even if they go to mass, even if they pray the Rosary at home, the culture is different. One parent may have gone to

Catholic school his whole life and is a regular mass attender. Another may have been baptized and made their First Communion and perhaps has attended mass irregularly since. And still another person in front of you might be the non-Catholic parent while the other works during the hours you offer programming. Some may have a complicated relationship with God, or with the Church, or with your pastor, but they want their children to know God, to have faith. They want them to have a foundation, to have traditions. They want them to pray.

PARENTHOOD AS CALLING

I had the privilege a few years ago of working with Vibrant Faith and the Lilly Endowment on a project focused on calling. The "Called to Lives of Meaning and Purpose Initiative," as they titled it, launched in 2018, generously funded by Lilly Endowment, Inc. The Initiative funded thirteen innovation hubs across North America, along with the Collegeville Institute, which served as our coordinator. (Hubs included Boston University, Samford University, Whitworth University, Baylor University, Regent College, Hope College, American Baptist College, Fuller Theological Seminary, Louisville Seminary, Virginia Theological Seminary, Samuel DeWitt Proctor Conference, Collegeville Institute, and Vibrant Faith.) The coordination effort at Collegeville Institute helped the hubs work with congregations to launch ministries that help Christians discover and claim how God is calling them to lead lives of meaning and purpose. Dr. Kathleen Cahalan of Collegeville Institute, author of *The Stories We Live: Finding God's Calling All Around Us*, walked with us, as needed, throughout the entire project.

At Vibrant Faith, we worked with twenty-four congregations across the country. I coached the leadership teams from four Catholic parishes in New Jersey, Wisconsin, and Oregon. All four parishes were engaged in family faith formation in some way. Their goal throughout this project was to develop ways they might help people discern how God was at work in their lives. What was he calling them from, through, and to? This was some of the most life-giving work I've ever done. I think the reason it felt so sacred to me was that I had the privilege of hearing the stories of people who are living out and growing in their faith. Some of my favorite stories were those of parents. I loved hearing how they saw God in their family, in their children, in their daily interactions.

So, what if we reimagined parent sessions? What if we focused on the relationship between parents and their children? On their calling to parenthood? Their calling as Mom or as Dad? For years I have spoken to families about my children, about my calling as a mother, about how my children have truly been my greatest spiritual directors. Sure, as a ministry leader I had spiritual directors through the years— and I in no way wish to diminish the work they've helped me do in my spiritual life—but the impact my children had on my spiritual life is almost immeasurable. I believe parenthood calls us deeply to who God created us to be. Parenting calls forth characteristics and values that lead us (or can lead us) closer to God. Parenthood teaches us about ourselves and about God.

"My children taught me to pray," I say, and then add, "to *really, really*, pray." And parents laugh. They know what I mean. If you are a parent, you have probably prayed to God more for your child—or about issues that arose around raising your children—than anything else. I know I have, and I don't believe that changes as they grow. The prayers change in nature, but we still pray for our children, and for theirs, our grandchildren. We know we need God's help.

My children taught me to be present. My youngest always lived in the moment. Not yesterday, not tomorrow: right now. You know the child who holds your face in their chubby little fingers and says, "Look at me, Mom!" Pay attention, they say. I was so much more aware of God's presence in our lives because of this little child. We experienced wonder and awe everywhere!

My children also taught me to surrender. I was a bit of a control freak before children. Not that I really believed I could control everything, but I sure tried. You learn quickly how little control you really have. I remember sending my first off to school and realizing there was a huge part of her day that I had no knowledge of. Sure, I knew who her teacher was. I knew where she was. But I did not know what her interactions were like. I couldn't be there to protect her if other kids were mean. I couldn't make sure she wasn't being mean. I had to surrender. But that was a tiny surrender compared to later years. We surrender them to the world again and again, as we allow them to go on field trips, to stay at someone else's house, as we send them out to drive with their new driver's license for the first time, to babysit, and especially as we send them off to college or their first full-time job.

I've shared these stories with parents. Then I get specific and walk them through my own examples. Like the time my eldest daughter was twelve and found a lump in her breast. Friends asked how I wasn't losing my mind. I was, a little, at the beginning, I said, but I thought I had to be strong for my daughter: then I realized how strong she was. I shared my prayer with them and asked them to pray with us. I told them how my daughter was teaching me to pray and to surrender it all to God. I had no control. I could only pray, "Lord, she's your child, too, your child first! Please be with her. Please be with us. Heal her. Heal me." We gave thanks for the gifts throughout the process: for the surgeons who removed the lump, for the knowledge that it was not cancer. We learned to pray together in a way I had not done when I was her age. I learned an inner strength and dependence on my faith that I'm not sure I knew before this moment.

My son announced in high school that he was going to West Point. As proud as I was that he got into the Academy, once again I turned to prayer. This mama's heart was not made to let go the way I would need to in the years to come. Again and again: first, as my son experienced a college life so different from his peers; then as he entered the Army after graduation; again as he went through Ranger school; and especially when he was deployed to the Middle East. In the years he was in the military, he and I both grew in our devotion to Mary, unbeknownst to each other. We've talked about it since. I'm not sure what his first attraction was, but I was focused on the mother who gave her Son to something greater than himself—a calling that God had prepared for him. The image of the *Pietà* was one that helped me see Mary's heartbreak but also her strength. The reason: Jesus had said, "Behold your mother." She was here for us in the most heart-wrenching moments, leading us to her Son.

I confess to parents that as a young Catholic mom, I struggled with Mary. I struggled with that image of perfection. "Full of grace." That does not describe my early days as a mom, at least not when I was in the midst of diapers, night feedings, night terrors, teething, and a living room that looked more like a daycare center. Three children in three years. I didn't sleep for years. I questioned how I was doing as a mom—not all the time, but a lot of the time. Looking back, I know it was God's grace that got us through, but I didn't know that then. I feel like knowing this would have helped. I wish my parish had offered me accompaniment in the way that so many parishes have offered moms support these last few years. I might not have stayed away from Mary for so long.

Parents can relate when you're honest. If you have always had a devotion to Mary, tell them why: not the Church knowledge "she's our Mother" reason, but the heart reason. What is it that drew you to Mary? How does she help you love her Son? How does she give you strength? As I've shared these stories and others with families, I create space for them to share with me and with one another how God has called them as a parent. We begin with easy questions: how many children they have, their ages, and so on. Then I ask, "What has most surprised you about parenting or becoming a parent?" Their answers are always so honest.

"I couldn't believe how I could function with so little sleep."

"I can't believe how different each of my children are."

"I can't believe how early they learned how to push my buttons."

"I can't believe how much my heart has expanded."

We always have at least one parent who shares this last one: the idea that they couldn't imagine how much they could love a child, and that they never imagined they could love the next child enough, but that love multiplies; it doesn't divide. "It's like God is teaching us how he loves," one dad said. Amen. Yes, God is teaching us what it's like to love unconditionally.

We ask parents to remember the first time they held their child:

- What did you think?
- What did you feel?
- What were your dreams?
- What were your fears?

And then we ask them to go a little deeper:

- What has your child taught you about life?
- About love?
- About prayer?
- About faith?
- About God?

And finally,

- How has God called you as a mom or a dad?

Their answers are so raw, so authentic. I still get emotional when I hear their responses as I participate in parent sessions that walk through these questions and focus on the parent's relationship with their children. I believe that the faith formation approaches of the future must help families discern God's movement in their lives. This is a parent session that will build relationships between parents in their small groups (or whoever they sit with) and with the leaders and the community. You are talking about what matters most to them in the whole world. You can't *not* love these parents after you've heard them talk about their children. The vulnerability opens them up to relationships with others, to talking about their relationship with God. But you also have to be authentic. And be vulnerable.

It's easy to set up an "us and them" relationship. It happens all too often in faith formation programs. In the beginning, I know I built a wall around myself. I didn't want to talk about my life, and especially not about my children. I suppose I wanted to protect myself from the parents' resistance to this change, from their judgment. When I worked as a director of lifelong faith formation in a parish that was starting to implement this new model, no one else in our area was offering family faith formation. Parents threatened to leave and go to neighboring churches. I wanted to play the "expert" and quote the Church and the research. I didn't want to let them in. I didn't want to open myself up to relationship. If I did, I knew it could get personal; I could get hurt. It could get messy. I didn't want messy. I was focused on expectations and boundaries and on running the program "the right way."

But our pastor knew better. Listen to them, he said. Affirm that we hear them. We might not go back to the way things were, he said, but we can hear their concerns. He knew that most concerns came from a place of fear. Most of that resistance came from a place of worrying that one was not a good enough Catholic, that we were going to quiz parents and find out what they didn't know, that we would shame them for all the things they didn't know or the ways they didn't practice the faith. Our pastor was determined to build relationships with these families.

Fr. Don Lewandowski, OSA, was an educator at heart. He had been a teacher, a principal, a DRE. I would not be in this ministry if not for him. For almost twelve years, we worked to build a program that was family centered and parent friendly. He affirmed families for what they were already doing well. "You have a greater chance of becoming a saint than I do!" he would say. "You become more like Christ every day as you do the things Jesus taught us to do."

Parents sacrifice for one another and for their children. Every day. In countless ways. Jesus taught us to sacrifice for the other. Parents forgive one another, and their children, and teach their children how to forgive in little ways and big ways. Jesus taught us the importance of forgiveness. In families we heal one another: whether it's putting Band-Aids on the boo-boos or listening to someone after a hard day at work or a stressful day at school. Jesus healed people and showed his disciples how to do the same. Parents pray for their children, even when they are struggling with their relationship with God or with the Church. If their child is sick, they pray, and they ask others to pray, too. Jesus taught us to pray and how to pray.

Fr. Don affirmed parents, made them feel better about the job they were doing, made them feel better about being Catholic. He invited them on a journey that was based on their own families and God's call to them as moms and dads. He affirmed the holiness that Pope Francis spoke of in Dublin, Ireland, at the 2018 World Meeting of Families when he said:

> It is called holiness. I like to speak of the saints "next door", all those ordinary people who reflect God's presence in the life and history of our world. The vocation to love and to holiness is not something reserved for a privileged few....It is silently present in the heart of all those families that offer love, forgiveness and mercy when they see the need, and do so quietly, without great fanfare. The Gospel of the family is truly joy for the world, since there, in our families, Jesus can always be found, dwelling in simplicity and poverty as he did in the home of the Holy Family of Nazareth.

Reimagining parent meetings (in a way that affirms parents) encourages a reflection of their call as Mom or as Dad, recognizes their holiness as a member of God's family, and honors their dignity. This can go a long way in empowering families to live their faith. We know from past experience (and from psychology) that shaming does not help—that focusing on what someone is not doing that they should be doing is a sure way to put distance between us and them. But walking with them where they are, focusing on what matters most to them (their children)—*that* can have an incredible impact on your ministry and thus on the faith formation of the children in your parish.

Questions for Reflection

1. Parents are being countercultural showing up, bringing their children for faith formation or for sacrament preparation. How can we affirm parents? How can we embolden them further to share their faith with their children and with the broader community?

2. What would be the benefits of reimagining parent meetings or parent gatherings in the way described?

3. Some people who have hesitated to implement family faith formation recognize the need of a supportive pastor but may not have one. How can you advocate for family faith formation in that case? How can a leader form his or her parish leadership and staff in the need to engage parents and all families?

4. What do you think would happen if you talked to parents about their dreams for their children? Their fears? What if you asked them what keeps them up at night? How might these questions build community?

5. What resonates in chapter 3? What challenges you?
Or what would you challenge?

The Church will have to initiate everyone—priests, religious and laity—into this "art of accompaniment" which teaches us to remove our sandals before the sacred ground of the other.

POPE FRANCIS,
EVANGELII GAUDIUM, #169

FOUR

Holy Listening: Sacred Ground

I've often described Fr. Don Lewandowski, OSA, as my Eli. Just as Samuel needed Eli to hear his calling (1 Samuel 3:1–10), I would not be in family ministry if it weren't for this man. I visited his office one day, curious about a rumor I had heard that the English teacher in our parish school was retiring. My children were still in the school, though only for one more year. Before I submitted my résumé, I wanted to make sure he had no objections about me teaching my youngest child during her last year in junior high. As I shared my experience and the reason I hadn't taught these last few years (my children), Fr. Don just smiled. Eventually, when I paused long enough, he simply said, "I have something else entirely in mind for you."

Fr. Don had visited two parishes that were offering family faith formation. What he knew about the research and statistics around the exodus of young people away from the Church, and what he saw in these parishes, convinced him of the need to make a change. He said families in those parishes—parents and children—were engaged. People were smiling. He saw dads: dads talking with their children, dads talking with each other, about faith. He said this gave him incredible hope. We talked about the youngest children, the infants and toddlers on parents' laps. What kind of impact would this have on those children? For years before they would participate in any faith formation directed at them, they would experience their parents in faith formation settings, talking about faith, teaching the faith, even living the faith. What incredible witness in those early years!

Fr. Don was convinced we had the opportunity to make a difference not just in the lives of children, but in the lives of the parents as well. This is holy work. This is why Pope Francis suggests that approaching another, accompanying another, is like approaching sacred ground. We had to see this new adventure as if we were walking on sacred ground.

For almost twelve years, I had the privilege of serving with and learning from Fr. Don. One of the greatest lessons (and there were many), as I alluded to in the last chapter, was listening: holy listening, active listening, listening that let people know they were seen; they were heard. "Listen to them," he said. "We will be better for it." He was right. We invited people to listening sessions. What were we getting right? What could we do better? What were they looking for? The listening we did—whether casual, in the hallway, or the narthex, or the parking lot, or in these listening sessions—made our program better.

We held multiple listening sessions each year. How can you do this? Personal invitation. We kept each session to groups of ten to twelve people. We invited a few parents or catechists whom we knew were supportive of this paradigm shift, but then we also invited a few who were the most vocal about resisting this change. Why? We needed to affirm that those who were resistant were heard, but we also needed them to hear other perspectives, and we needed to not be the only people pushing for parent inclusion in our programs. I may not have changed every mind, but I know that every person who walked away felt heard. I also know that many of the most resistant brought perspectives to us that helped us make the program better. We might not have thought of that non-Catholic parent who would be in attendance when the Catholic parent was working. We might not have thought of that single parent who couldn't always work around our days/times. By listening to these parents, we not only remembered to welcome the non-Catholic in the room, we knew we needed to plan, even program, for this parent as well. What if we offered a session on parents who believe differently or who practice their faith differently (which could also include two Catholic parents)? By listening to these parents, we also created an option for "family faith angels." Here, parents who wanted their children in faith formation but couldn't necessarily be available every time, due to extenuating circumstances, could partner with family faith angels—persons who could bring the child and work with the parent at home so that the parent could provide support to the child throughout the month at home and in the community.

Creating a culture of listening might be the first step a parish makes on its journey toward a family-centered approach to faith formation. If you've read Sherry Weddell's *Forming Intentional Disciples*, you know that the first threshold of conversion is trust. We can't expect parents to be open and ready to share unless we build those bonds of trust. Daniel Coyle, author of *The Culture Code*, says, "Vulnerability doesn't come after trust, it precedes it." So, it seems we might need to be willing to be vulnerable first.

There are many reasons we need to rebuild trust. It becomes clear to me how important Gospel accompaniment is in these times. Pope Francis has been encouraging us to practice this kind of accompaniment, but it's not new. Throughout Scripture and our Catholic Tradition, we have many examples of accompaniment, of one person journeying with another, helping them attend to God's presence in their lives: Elijah and Elisha, Eli and Samuel, Ruth and Naomi, Mary and Elizabeth, Jesus and his disciples, St. Francis De Sales and St. Jane de Chantal, St. Francis of Assisi and St. Clare, St. Catherine and Pope Gregory. The list goes on. It seems this kind of journeying together makes a difference in the lives of God's people.

Reimagining faith formation, then, might best be found at this intersection of calling, storytelling and story listening, and accompaniment. Erik Samuelson, my friend and colleague at Vibrant Faith, asks, "Could listening be our greatest service as ministry leaders?" He often quotes philosopher and theologian Douglas Steere, who wrote: "To 'listen' another's soul into a condition of disclosure and discovery may be almost the greatest service that any human being ever performs for another." Erik calls this "Holy Listening." It's the kind of listening that involves our whole being. We're not distracted. We're not worried about how we're going to respond. We listen to the other as if it's Scripture. How is God going to show up?

This kind of listening is an act of love. This kind of listening encourages the other to share their story. Perhaps this is where we've failed in the past in ministry to families. We've spoken, we've talked, or we've lectured. We've stated what our expectations are. But have we listened? Have we asked what they're looking for? And then really listened? Have we created space for storytelling and story listening so that we might be empowering and equipping people to share their faith stories with their children and with one another?

Pope Francis has often talked about a "listening Church." He emphasizes creating this culture of listening as he invites us on a synodal journey. "The path of synodality is the path that God expects from the Church of the third millennium," he says in his 2015 address commemorating the 50th Anniversary of the Institution of the Synod of Bishops. A synodal Church is a Church which listens, which realizes that listening "is more than simply hearing." He continues, "It is a mutual listening in which everyone has something to learn. The faithful people, the college of bishops, the Bishop of Rome: all listening to each other, and all listening to the Holy Spirit, the 'Spirit of truth' (John 14:17), in order to know what he 'says to the Churches' (Revelation 2:7)."

Listening is an essential quality of an authentic parent ministry. Our faith suggests that when we are present to one another in this way, there our Lord is with us. "For where two or three are gathered together in my name, there am I in the midst of them" (Matthew 18:20).

Questions for Reflection

1. Who has been Eli for you, helping you hear your call? Who have you accompanied in that listening journey?

2. Pope Francis talks about a "listening Church." What might that look like in your setting?

3. Did your parish participate in synodal listening sessions in preparation for the 2023 synod? If so, what did you hear? How will you affirm that participants were heard?

4. If you did not participate in synodal listening sessions, why not?

5. Could listening be our greatest service as ministry leaders? Why or why not?

6. If trust is the first threshold of conversion, how do you build trust in your ministry?

7. How might you hold listening sessions to help plan for, design, or implement a family-friendly faith formation approach? If you currently offer such an approach, how have you included listening (to parents and catechists) as part of your discernment in the past? How might you include this kind of listening moving forward?

8. What resonates in chapter 4? What challenges you? Or what would you challenge?

PART THREE

Where to Begin

Believing parents, with their daily example of life, have the most effective capacity to transmit the beauty of the Christian faith to their children. "Enabling families to take up their role as active agents of the family apostolate calls for 'an effort at evangelization and catechesis inside the family.'" The greatest challenge in this situation is for couples, mothers and fathers, active participants in catechesis, to overcome the mentality of delegation that is so common, according to which the faith is set aside for specialists in religious education. This mentality is, at times, fostered by communities that struggle to organize family centered catechesis which starts from the families themselves.

DIRECTORY FOR CATECHESIS, #124

FIVE

Prayer, Formation, and Vision

Answering a challenge given by Monsignor Ray East of the Archdiocese of Washington, D.C., at the national Fashion Me a People conference, St. Jude's Faith Formation Board began studying the bishops' pastoral plan *Our Hearts Were Burning Within Us* (USCCB). "Change two things," said Monsignor East, "and it will change the culture of your parish and transform your leadership."

He was talking about placing an intentional focus on prayer and forming parish leaders in the Church's vision of the new evangelization. He was adamant that giving prayer and formation twenty minutes at every meeting would result in transformation. I couldn't imagine adding more time to meetings that already seemed to go on forever some nights. Still, we accepted the challenge. We committed to one year, started every meeting with a modified *lectio divina* focused on the upcoming Sunday's gospel, then continued with twenty minutes of reading and discussing *Our Hearts Were Burning Within Us.*

We experienced the power of prayer in this practice. Praying together, intentionally, with the Church's prayer, focused on the upcoming Sunday's Gospel, changed our meetings immediately. It softened our hearts. It united us, allowed us to see different perspectives, helped us to get to know one another: our lives, our struggles, our celebrations. We weren't just people with agendas. We weren't just focused on the business of ministry. We were sisters and brothers in Christ, focused on the mission of the Church.

Formation took more time. We spent over two years reading and reflecting on *Our Hearts Were Burning Within Us*. Most months, the conversations were lively and engaging; in twenty minutes, we might get through only two or three paragraphs. This experience was essential in the designing of our lifelong faith formation approach. A number of ideas resonated with us, but the notion that adult formation would be beneficial to the children and youth of our community just made sense. "An adult community whose faith is well-formed and lively will more effectively pass that faith on to the next generation. Moreover, the witness of adults actively continuing their own formation shows children and youth that growth in faith is lifelong and does not end upon reaching adulthood" (OHWB, #40).

FOCUSING ON ADULT FAITH FORMATION IS BENEFICIAL TO CHILDREN'S FAITH FORMATION

Forming parents results in formed children. When we first started implementing family programming at St. Jude, a few board members thought parish leaders were just trying to mix things up, implementing change for the purpose of change. But after reading and studying this pastoral plan, they saw the Church's vision for how parish communities could flourish, how we could become "vitally alive" communities. Thus, our reading and reflection led the board to give primary emphasis to adult faith. We needed not just to offer adult formation but to imagine how we might put it at the forefront of our catechetical efforts:

> Adult faith formation, by which people consciously grow in the life of Christ through experience, reflection, prayer, and study, must be "the central task in [this] catechetical enterprise," becoming "the axis around which revolves the catechesis of childhood and adolescence as well as that of old age." This can

be done specifically through developing in adults a better understanding of and participation in the full sacramental life of the Church. (OHWB, #5)

Focused on this vision, the section of the pastoral plan that impacted our conversation the most was the emphasis on parish life. The parish, then, provides the place, persons, and means to summon and sustain adults in lifelong conversion of heart, mind, and life. It is, "without doubt, the most important locus in which the Christian community is formed and expressed" (OHWB, #117). The bishops said, "The Parish Is the Curriculum! While this pastoral plan is concerned primarily with intentional adult faith formation programs, the success of such efforts rests very much on the quality and total fabric of parish life" (OHWB, #118).

So, what if we looked at the parish as curriculum? What would that look like? We started with an appreciative inquiry in the parish and assessed what was working. What was already happening in the life of the parish that might give parishioners an opportunity to encounter Christ? What if we created a network of formation and evangelization with the ministry leaders who were already passionate about sharing their personal faith and our Catholic faith in their ministries? The "what if" questions began to inspire a dream, a vision of what a parish "vitally alive" might look like. This was the start of a holistic approach to reimagining faith formation as having multiple components, including electives.

Our board continued this process of prayer and formation through the years. Formation in the Church's instructions continued with *Amoris Laetitia* and *Evangelii Gaudium*. I described this "life of the parish" component in chapter 2, but I thought it important to share here how a parish might discern their vision, their goals.

When I coach parish teams through this kind of paradigm shift, I recommend a process of prayer and formation for the leadership team. *Our Hearts Were Burning Within Us* is still a relevant document for such formation, but today I recommend beginning with the *Directory for*

Catechesis, from the Pontifical Council for the Promotion of the New Evangelization, which Pope Francis approved in March 2020.

A parish leader could do this in a number of ways. First, determine who should be around the table. Is there a faith formation team, paid or unpaid? Will you include lead catechists? Pastoral staff? A faith formation board or commission? Once you've determined who the team is, decide what you will study together. You could read the *Directory for Catechesis* in full or in sections. Study guides, highlights, and summaries are available for catechists. You could even focus entirely on chapter 8: "Catechesis in the Lives of Persons." If you do this, I would include the footnote material that is supportive of this section. For example, the section on family catechesis also references *Redemptor Hominis*, *Familiaris Consortio*, *Amoris Laetitia*, the *General Directory for Catechesis*, and *Evangelii Gaudium*. What a great way to take a long look at what the Church teaches about families, catechesis, and evangelization!

VISION

After you've grounded yourself in prayer and formation, you are probably anxious to jump right in. Before you do, take time to process that formation so you begin with a strong vision for your parish. Why change your faith formation program? What are your reasons? What are your goals? We need to start with a destination in mind if we're going to design a plan to get there. I often begin with an appreciative inquiry, asking the parish, "What do you love about your community? What's working? What are you known for? What is your charism?"

Ask, "What if?" Let yourself sit with that. "What if" is a profound reframing. If resources were not an issue, what would your program look like? What is your dream for your families? What is your prayer for the children of the parish? Articulate that vision. Be clear. Be concise, because you will need to share that vision, and people will need to understand what you mean when you announce a shift toward family faith, or intergenerational faith, or lifelong faith formation, or whatever approach you discern. Sharing that vision will require communication, communication, communication! Just as the team was allowed a period of prayer and formation, your community will need that same allowance.

Questions for Reflection

1. Who do you collaborate with? Who's around the table? How do you build that team?

2. How does your team pray together?

3. How do you form your team in a vision of faith formation that engages every family?

4. Do you have an articulated vision for faith formation for your parish? If you do, as you review it, does it articulate what you would want it to say? If it does not, how might you change it?

5. If you do not have an articulated vision for your faith formation program, what steps will you take to create one?

6. Once you have articulated your vision, how might you share that vision and build support for it in your parish?

7. Where does "what if" lead you?

8. What resonates in chapter 5? What challenges you? Or what would you challenge?

The parish is not an outdated institution; precisely because it possesses great flexibility, it can assume quite different contours depending on the openness and missionary creativity of the pastor and the community....If the parish proves capable of self-renewal and constant adaptivity, it continues to be "the Church living in the midst of the homes of her sons and daughters". This presumes that it really is in contact with the homes and the lives of its people, and does not become a useless structure out of touch with people or a self-absorbed group made up of a chosen few....In all its activities the parish encourages and trains its members to be evangelizers. It is a community of communities, a sanctuary where the thirsty come to drink in the midst of their journey, and a center of constant missionary outreach. We must admit, though, that the call to review and renew our parishes has not yet sufficed to bring them nearer to people, to make them environments of living communion and participation, and to make them completely mission-oriented.

POPE FRANCIS, *EVANGELII GAUDIUM, #28*

SIX

Designing for Families

If the parish possesses great flexibility, can we be bold enough to review and renew the parish, as Pope Francis suggests? One size does not fit all. There is no cookie-cutter program to take off the shelf and implement as the "big fix." This *does* take commitment and work, but I can tell you it is life-giving work. Maintenance might seem easier, at first glance. It might feel like returning to order, going back to the "way we've always done it," but when we've seen the statistics, when we've become aware of the research, when we know young people are leaving as soon as they've been confirmed, if not before, doesn't that work feel like heavy lifting? Doesn't it feel futile? I choose the life-giving work.

So, where do we begin to design a family-friendly approach? After we've articulated our vision, we have a kind of map of where we want to go; now we have to determine what might best get us there. Review the appreciative inquiry. Keep in mind the gifts of the community. Then begin to survey the methods of faith formation that fit your vision.

There are many surveys of models out there. They review the strengths and challenges of each one. I will review some here, but this will not be as comprehensive as some surveys that will be referenced in the resource section of this book. Determine the model that best fits your parish, your vision, your leadership.

MODELS
- Parish classroom model: In this model, weekly instruction is offered to children by age or grade level.

- Summer model: The summer model is similar to the classroom model but is condensed into two or three weeks in the summertime for an intensive or immersive version.
- At-home model: This model is most often a homeschooling type of instruction. The parent is the primary instructor. Materials may be provided by the parish.
- Catechesis of the Good Shepherd model: Based on the Montessori method, this is hands-on religious education. A key component is the "Atrium"—a space dedicated to the children's exploration.
- Family model: Most family-based models include one week with families gathered for a learning session and three weeks where learning takes place at home.
- Intergenerational model: Here, gatherings provide multi-age learning for the whole faith community.
- Liturgical or lectionary-based model: This model offers lessons that correlate to the Sunday readings, helping families prepare for or celebrate liturgical celebrations in the church.

Within these models are various strategies or methods to customize an approach or combine multiple approaches.

First, your family approach might be gathered in person, or it might be online, or it could be hybrid, combining the best of both strategies. A family model could employ the flipped classroom model as a strategy, when appropriate, providing content for families to explore before the gathered session, then unpacking the learning or using the newly learned concepts or skills in the gathered session. A family model could also employ a lectionary-based approach. Most models can offer synchronous learning (at this time, in this place) and asynchronous learning (self-guided, on one's own time, but could have a due date). So, as your parish discerns the best model for you, keep in mind that this can be customized.

Some archdiocesan or diocesan offices offer guidelines for parish catechetical leaders. Choose your model, or customize a parish model, but include these essential components. For example, the Archdiocese of New York leaves the question of choosing a model of faith formation to the parish but offers twelve essential components each parish model must include.[6]

I would suggest that a model that engages every family should embrace the lessons we've explored in this book:

- parents as the primary witnesses of the faith to their children
- Sunday liturgy and other communal opportunities for praise and worship
- employing the best of technology in our delivery of faith formation content
- an emphasis on God-talk and faith practices, integrating multiple components to include gathered opportunities for parents and children
- home lessons
- community outreach or service
- allowing some autonomy regarding one's family faith formation plan
- embracing storytelling strategies

As you design that faith formation plan for your parish, survey what you need by following these eight steps:

1. Assess the formation you've done for your team and for the parish community.
2. Assess your vision.
3. Discern the best model for your community. How might you customize it according to your needs and the needs of your families?
4. Assess how you will employ listening strategies to ensure you hear those needs.

---

6   https://archny.org/wp-content/uploads/models-religious-education-glossy-1.pdf

5. Determine your best communication platforms and how you will use those throughout this paradigm shift. Determine what you will communicate and which person(s) will be responsible for that communication.
6. Determine what resources you will need: primarily, staff and volunteers, time, materials, and space.
7. Create a long-term schedule for implementing your vision, perhaps clearly stating the goals of year one through year five.
8. Plan for quick wins in the early years.

What do I mean by "quick wins"? There are ways you can begin to implement a family-centered approach to faith formation without turning everything upside down. One way is to begin sharing the formation: sharing with the parish and within the faith formation community the vision, the reasons you are moving toward this approach, while infusing family-friendly events throughout the year (seasonal family or intergenerational events, like a Advent family wreath-making event or an intergenerational Lenten event that includes an exploration of the three key Lenten practices: praying, fasting, and almsgiving).

A side note: In the beginning, people will ask, "What is mandatory?" I have never liked that question. If we say a child can miss two classes in a drop-off model, what's the likelihood that they will miss two classes? Pretty high. When we set up an expectation of the bare minimum, that is what we will get. Instead, I have always shared the banquet of faith formation opportunities we are providing for the families. I say, "We know your child's faith formation is important to you. You're here! This is what we commit to providing to you, for your family. We *hope and expect* that you will commit to every opportunity, every component offered." We explain that this is how the child (or the family) will get the most out of what is offered. We all know that you get out of something what you put into it. Positive language and positive attitude go a long way. We found that when a person missed more than one event or expectation, we then had the opportunity to be in dialogue with that family to discover what was happening that prevented them from participating. Quite often it was an opportunity to practice accompaniment. This built trust and relationships.

Another quick win is implementing a family approach in your sacrament preparation programs. These are special moments when the family is invested in a particular way. Parents are more open to participating—and often quite willing to participate—in this preparation. A quick win could also be the addition of a parallel parent group. This could be offered for all parents, or just the parents of children preparing for a sacrament, or just parents of teens, or parents of young children. You're "shrinking" the long-term goal by implementing a smaller one.

Also, look to the resources that are out there that will assist you in designing your plan. When I started out, there were few resources to look to; now there are many! The publishers of children's curriculums have added resources. There are resources specific to a family approach. In earlier chapters, we explored some of the diocesan and parish efforts that have provided resources for other communities. There are also websites that curate the best resources available, and some offer training as well (some for free, some at a minimal cost): lifelongfaith.com, catholicfamilyfaith.org, vibrant-faith-catalyst. mn.co, and my own: familieslivingfaith.com.

Finally, partner with others regionally or virtually. There's a lot of truth in the old saying that "If you want to get there fast, go alone, but if you want to go far, go together." Networking with others who are on a similar path, even if they are further ahead or way behind, offers some energy, and some brainstorming space, that encourages creativity. This is not a solo ministry. Expand your team outside of your parish.

Questions for Reflection

1. What from this chapter sparks curiosity?

2. Is there any resistance that rises within you?
If so, where does it come from?

3. If not resistance, is there anything that is still challenging you?

4. What encourages you?

5. What will you hang on to? What do you need to let go of?

6. What resonates in chapter 6? What challenges you?
Or what would you challenge?

Concluding Ideas and Opportunities for Further Discussion

To be effective ministers of adult faith formation we will first, like Jesus, join people in their daily concerns and walk side by side with them....We will ask them questions and listen attentively as they speak of their joys, hopes, griefs, and anxieties.

USCCB, *OUR HEARTS WERE BURNING WITHIN US, #8*

SEVEN

A Few Final Thoughts

This book is by no means a comprehensive exploration of how to engage families. I know I will look back and think, "I should have included this." Or "How did I forget that?" Still, I pray that it has offered you hope and encouragement. I pray you give yourself permission to dream, to experiment, to be vulnerable, and to open yourself up to new relationships. On a practical note, I hope it has provided ideas, solutions, and fodder for conversation as you design your own program.

This may sound like a lot of work. I'm not going to lie. It is. But it is life-giving work. Paradigm change is not easy, but the results are transformative: for the families, the parish, and for you, the leader. I know too many leaders in the Church who feel like their efforts are in vain, who know what we're doing in faith formation in many places is not working, and even one who said, "I feel like I'm banging my head against the wall." It might *seem* easy to continue to direct programs we've run the same way we've done it for years, but at what cost? It's exhausting to feel like we aren't making a difference, like we're barely planting seeds, and we're unsure if there's any one left to water them. This is what leads to burn out. Yes, change is hard. It's important that you do not try to do this alone. It is not a one-person job. It takes an entire team; it takes the whole community. You need a supportive pastor. If your pastor does not share your vision, advocate for the vision; form your staff in the reality we face today (the statistics and research I shared at the beginning). Help them see the possibilities you see. And trust the Holy Spirit. When you see families pray together more often, parents more comfortable in their role as the primary spiritual leader in the family, and families out in the community *living* their faith, you will know it was worth it.

Patrice Spirou, of the Archdiocese of Atlanta, shared this with me, "The biggest challenge is having patience with the process of converting hearts and minds to see the value of evangelizing a child's whole family rather than just teaching an individual student. It's a campaign, a team effort and it requires ongoing messaging, but that's how the Church got started right?!" She reminds her leaders that success requires commitment. "A paradigm shift is a marathon not a sprint."

I also want to reiterate what I said in the beginning. I have witnessed nothing less than courageous leadership throughout this pandemic. Leaders were resilient, adaptive, responsive, and flexible. They were creative, innovative, and inspiring. The future of faith formation will depend on this kind of adaptive leadership.

Tod Bolsinger, author of *Canoeing the Mountains: Christian Leadership in Uncharted Territory*, says, "Leadership is energizing a community of people toward their own transformation in order to accomplish a shared mission in the face of changing the world." We are in uncharted territory. What got us here won't get us where we want to go. I love Bolsinger's metaphor, using the story of Lewis and Clark reaching the Continental Divide, looking at the Rocky Mountains before them, and realizing they needed to ditch the canoe. Although it had gotten them to that point, it wasn't going to take them over the mountains. They had to listen to the people of the land, who could teach them what would come next.

Adaptive leadership will require listening, will require engaging the people we serve, so that we are actually shoulder to shoulder, working toward a new future together. I pray you will be a listening partner to those you serve. That you hear the "joys, hopes, griefs, and anxieties" and respond with love. I pray you have a heart for parents, that they might embrace their role to be the primary witnesses of faith for their children.

We *are* in uncharted territory, but I believe this liminal space will inspire creativity that will spark the renewal of the Church. *Come, Holy*

Spirit! And I believe we need to trust in that prayer...trust in the Spirit. Too often, we believe we are responsible for the faith of young people. In a sense, we are responsible for providing the opportunities for faith formation, but we are just the instruments our God uses to enliven this mission. It is God who initiates faith, who initiates the relationship, who invites us all into communion with our God who is relationship: Father, Son, and Holy Spirit. I have been guilty of taking credit for the numbers attending a program or taking the blame for a program's failure to launch. But it is not about me. I do need to give my all, to make myself available to the Spirit in this mission. Then I need to surrender it in prayer.

A final note: I began writing this book about eight years ago when my husband and I were on a road trip to Down East Maine celebrating our upcoming twenty-fifth wedding anniversary. Through the years, I would pick this project up and put it down again and again. This fall we returned to Maine and I started re-reading a book I had started on our previous trip, Christina Lemieux's *How to Catch a Lobster in Down East Maine.* Lemieux shares stories about her childhood, her community, and her way of living fishing for lobster. It may sound strange, but as I read her story, (both times) I found similarities to the Catholic Church and faith formation.

Lemieux says, "In these parts, lobster fishing is not just an occupation—it's a way of life and a family tradition. Children grow up "playing" lobster fishing in old skiffs parked in their parents' front yards." As I read this, I thought of Catholicism being a way of life, of the way children of past generations (and maybe a few today) "played mass." The author goes on:

> Lobster fishing is not a skill learned in school; rather, it is a vocation handed down from generation to generation, as son works alongside his father. Of the fishermen I surveyed for this book, 85 percent are part of a generation of lobster fishermen. Most of these fishermen had a father and a grandfather who worked as lobster fishermen and taught them the craft;

40 percent also had a lobster-fishing great-grandfather. One of my survey respondents came from five generations of lobster fishermen.

Throughout the book, Lemieux speaks of a life that is caught, a life one is immersed in, a way of being that just becomes the fabric of life. In past generations people grew up Catholic, immersed in homes that embodied Catholicism in statues of saints, images of Jesus on the wall, the rosary on Grandma's dresser, candles in the living room, the way people prayed before meals, and before bed, and the walk to the local parish on Sunday. Sure, this might not be the way everyone came to Catholicism. Others join the Church today through the Rite of Christian Initiation. Even then, there is a process of mentorship, of walking together with one who is further on the journey, that mimics this "handing down" of a way of life, that mimics Jesus sending disciples out two by two. As I read Lemieux's book, I kept reflecting on these realities. Catholicism is "not a skill learned in school." It is a life that is caught, through modeling, through immersion, through repetition, day in and day out ways of living the faith.

In *Holy Work with Children*, Dr. Tanya Campen also speaks of this realization that we must move away from what she calls a "banking pedagogy." Campen says:

> "[I]t assumes that by depositing information into a young person's brain it will have an impact on the child. This approach to learning developed out of a rich history of Christian education....This form of education focused on transferring knowledge, and therefore the curriculum focused on lecturing, memorization, and tests.

Campen says by doing this we often fail to develop wonder and encourage discovery:

We forget that faith is a life-long process, we neglect the call to help people of all ages develop their own capacities for spiritual formation, and we abandon the call for relational ministry of any kind. Banking pedagogy therefore contributes to an oppressive narrative, one that is built on giving persons faith and telling them what to believe instead of creating a space where the Holy Spirit can move freely, helping persons develop their individual faith narratives in relationship with others through active wondering, critical thinking, reflection, and discovery.

As I reflected last year on the desire of some to return to the classroom, I knew it was time to tell this story. We must create communities where Catholicism is a way of life, where like a lobster fishing community we are passing faith on from one generation to the next through a lived experience, not a banking pedagogy, depositing information. I believe this will happen through equipping and empowering families to live the faith in the home and in the community. We cannot continue to offer models that are disconnected from family and the parish community. To create a space where the Spirit can move freely is to trust the Spirit to soften the hearts of our people and draw them closer to our God. And because our God has taken the initiative, we can be bold, as Pope Francis implored. Be bold and ask, "What if?"

Let every dawn find us courageous.
AMANDA GORMAN

Prayer

Good and Gracious God,
we grieve so much loss these last couple of years:
loved ones, jobs, isolation, polarization in our Church
    and our world.
Please heal our pain and mend our brokenness.
We do not know what changes we've experienced that
    will persist into the future,
still, we offer thanks for your presence through it all,
    for your steadfast love.

We thank you for the privilege of walking with families,
of hearing their stories and learning how they have seen you
    at work in their lives.
Bless our efforts to bring families together,
and to equip and empower parents to lead their children
    to follow you in faith.

We thank you too for an experience of Church that we hope
    renews our collective hunger for Eucharist
and calls us to nourish those in need.
May this experience leave us desiring and ever working
    for community.

We give thanks for creativity and innovation, for new ardor,
    new methods, and new expressions.
We ask you to guide us, inspire us, and renew us
that we might in turn renew our faith communities.

Amen.

ACKNOWLEDGMENTS

My eternal gratitude goes out to the many people who made this book possible.

To my editors, Heidi Busse and Ann Louise Mahoney: For your patience, your hard work, and dedication to this project—thank you. You advocated for this message. You made this stream of conscience rambling readable for its audience. Thank you for your wisdom and experience. I am forever in your debt.

To my dear friends in ministry—mentors and colleagues, leaders in parish and diocesan offices, in non-profit organizations, speakers, and writers in your own right, some of you named in the pages that preceded this, some unnamed, you know who you are: You have inspired me, formed me, comforted me, and challenged me. You have created the space for me to be authentically me, broken and flawed, but ever hopeful that I am answering God's call. For your accompaniment on this journey, your grace of spirit, generosity of time, and witness to God's love—thank you. Thank you for reminding me to allow God to surprise me. Words are not enough.

To the professors at Catholic Theological Union, and the visiting professors I had the privilege to learn from, thank you, for teaching me to wonder, to explore, to go deeper in the text. Thank you also for inspiring projects that became the research for first drafts of this book. I am ever grateful for my education at CTU.

To the families who inspired this passion for family faith formation, the parents who taught me what it would look like to walk with them, who shared their stories of new life and loss, of the wonder of raising children and the difficulty of letting them go, of the day-in and day-out moments they saw God in their own children and in their own lives: I thank you for the privilege of walking toward Christ together. Thank you for showing me how, for opening me up, allowing me to be vulnerable, and teaching me to focus on the person God places in front of me, here and now, in each moment.

And finally, to my own family—the chosen family, the married-into, born-into, and made family:

To my chosen sisters (and their spouses), my BMS Girls—Body Mind and Spirit(s), who were my "bubble-wrap" in the early years of this paradigm shift, protecting me so I wouldn't break, making it possible for me to keep on going, the ladies who volunteered at parish faith festivals in support of this vision (and me), who took me away for weekends to reflect on and talk of God's love and how God might be at work in our lives, who read *The Shack* out loud with me one weekend and pondered, "What is God really like?" who are my cheerleaders still to this day, even as I beg off get-togethers to work, and speak, and write: Thank you! Thank you for loving me, no matter what. Thank you for the privilege of loving you back. Your friendship is one of God's greatest gifts in my life.

To my married-into family, my husband's family who showed him what love looks like, who formed him into the man he is today: Thank you! How I love you and this man that you made! The way you taught him to treasure family, to love food and drink and gathering around the table. Your influence on him continues into the generations. Memories are made again and again as we feast together.

To my siblings who were witnesses to my childhood and have become great friends in our adult years, and to their partners who put up with it all. Thank you for sharing memories past and committing to making new ones as we all move to the same city for the first time since childhood. I am ever grateful for the gift of my sister and brother, life partners from our first days!

To my parents who taught me what love is, what it looks like up close. Thank you for your sacrifice for and commitment to one another and to us, with almost sixty years of marriage, you are an incredible inspiration! Thank you, Mom and Dad, for instilling in us a love of the written word, a love of storytelling and story listening. Thank you for supporting me in too many ways to list.

And especially to my husband Rob and the family we've made. As I said at the beginning, this is dedicated to you. Anyone in ministry knows, it is the family who sacrifices and makes it possible for a ministry leader to be present to his or her ministry. You all are my strength. I love you.

RESOURCES

BOOKS

Benner, David. *Sacred Companions: The Gift of Spiritual Friendship and Direction*. Downers Grove, IL: InterVarsity Press, 2002.

Bolsinger, Tod. *Canoeing the Mountains: Christian Leadership in Uncharted Territory*. Downers Grove, IL: InterVarsity Press, 2018.

Cahalan, Kathleen. *The Stories We Live: Finding God's Calling All Around Us*. Grand Rapids, MI: Eerdmans, 2017.

Camille, Alice. *Listening to God's Word*. Maryknoll, NY: Orbis, 2009.

Campen, Tanya. *Holy Work with Children: Making Meaning Together*. Eugene, OR: Wipf and Stock, 2021.

Committee on Evangelization and Catechesis. *Outreach to the Unaffiliated*. Washington, D.C.: United States Conference of Catholic Bishops, 2020.

Coyle, Daniel. *The Culture Code: The Secrets of Highly Successful Groups*. New York: Bantam Books, 2018.

Isay, Dave. *Listening Is an Act of Love*. New York: Penguin Books, 2007.

Manion, Jeff. *The Land Between: Finding God in Difficult Transitions*. Grand Rapids, MI: Zondervan, 2012.

McCarty, Robert. *Going, Going, Gone: The Dynamics of Disaffiliation in Young Catholics*. Winona, MN: St. Mary's Press, 2017.

Pontifical Council for the Promotion of the New Evangelization. *Directory for Catechesis: A Guide to the Proclamation of the Gospel by the Christian Faithful*. Washington, D.C.: United States Conference of Catholic Bishops, 2020.

Pope Francis. *Let Us Dream: The Path to a Better Future*. New York: Simon & Schuster, 2020.

———. *Christ Is Alive (Christus Vivit)*. Washington, D.C.: United States Conference of Catholic Bishops, 2019.

———. *The Joy of the Gospel (Evangelii Gaudium)*. Washington, D.C.: United States Conference of Catholic Bishops, 2016.

———. *The Joy of Love (Amoris Laetitia)*. Washington, D.C.: United States Conference of Catholic Bishops, 2016.

Rohr, Richard (and others). *Oneing, Liminal Space*. Albuquerque, NM: Center for Action and Contemplation, 2020.

Smith, Christian, and Melinda Lundquist Denton. *Soul Searching: The Religious and Spiritual Lives of American Teenagers*. New York: Oxford University Press, 2009.

Stanton, Brandon. *Humans of New York: Stories*. New York: St. Martin's Press, 2015.

United States Conference of Catholic Bishops. *Our Hearts Were Burning Within Us*. Washington, D.C.: United States Conference of Catholic Bishops, 1999.

Weddell, Sherry. *Forming Intentional Disciples: The Path to Knowing and Following Jesus*. Huntington, IN: Our Sunday Visitor, 2012.

WEBSITES FOR CATECHETICAL LEADERS

Strong Catholic Family Faith provides parish and school leaders with high quality resources to equip and empower the Catholic family at catholicfamilyfaith.org.

John Roberto is committed to helping churches develop lifelong faith formation for all ages and generations at lifelongfaith.com.

Vibrant Faith's Catalyst is a network of leaders committed to vibrant, transformational faith in Jesus—lived out in community! Check it out at http://vibrant-faith-catalyst.mn.co/.

The author's website, **Families Living Faith**, is dedicated to supporting leaders committed to walking with families in faith: familieslivingfaith.com.